A Modern Herbal

A Modern Herbal

How to Grow, Cook and use Herbs

Edited by
Violet Stevenson

TREASURE PRESS

ACKNOWLEDGEMENTS

Illustrations by Elsie Wrigley and David Bryant
Cookery photography by Roger Phillips

Grateful acknowledgement is made to:
Coach House Herbs,
Norton-sub-Hamden,
Somerset

Hereford Herbs,
Ocle Pychard,
Herefordshire.

who provided the herbs for the cookery.

Also to Mrs Maxwell of the American Museum at Bath

Photographs courtesy of
Leslie Johns
A-Z Botanical Collection
Ardea
Bodleian Library
Spectrum

First published by Cathay Books
This edition published by Treasure Press
59 Grosvenor Street
London W1

© 1974 Lynx Press Limited

ISBN 0 907407 13 7

Printed in Hong Kong

CONTENTS

In the Beginning

Anyone can have an interest in herbs, whether he or she is a gardener or a cook or one who enjoys merely their fragrance. Most people will probably enjoy all of these aspects, but you do not necessarily need a garden in order to grow herbs and you do not have to cook them in order to obtain pleasure from them. There's more to herbs than mint, sage, thyme and parsley, though many people's experience does not go beyond these four. How much more interesting cooking, growing and using herbs become if one makes use of their full variety.

First, naturally, one asks what is a herb. Technically, and to quote the Royal Horticultural Society Dictionary of Gardening, a herb is 'a plant of which the stem dies to the ground at the end of the season. Herbs may be annual, biennial or perennial'. So you see by this token no shrubs or trees are herbs in the botanical sense. Yet some shrubs, thyme and rosemary for example, and at least one tree, the sweet bay, are among our most important and savoury 'herbs'. Obviously the botanical meaning of the word is not enough. To the layman and by

Far left: An illustration of common mallow, Malva sylvestris, *from an old book of herbs. In the tradition of herbal illustrations, the drawing is delicate and beautifully clear.*

Top left: Garden angelica. Bottom left: Wild angelica. *Both illustrations from the 16th Century* Gerarde Herbal. *Above: A fenced-in herb garden from the 16th Century* Book of Hours.

general consent the term is used most often to describe those plants with savours which improve the quality of food, as well as certain others with scented and pleasing foliage such as southernwood and lavender. But the term has also a wider significance.

Many herbs also have a medicinal value, once held in great esteem and still valid in this day of manufactured drugs. For centuries the cultivation of these particular plants was of great importance, so much so that eventually they helped to shape our gardens.

At one time herbs were both widely gathered from the countryside and cultivated in gardens. Medicinal plants were dried so that they might be available at all times of the year and in places other than those where they could be expected to grow freely. It is interesting that our word 'drug' is simply part of the Anglo-Saxon verb 'drigan', to dry. And, apart from medicine, many plants were used magically, among other things as love potions, aphrodisiacs, to thwart the devil and witches, to add power to a curse, even to stop a dog barking at you!

Ancient Greece

So ancient is the cult and use of herbs that it is impossible to trace their earliest history. Certainly we know from the records they left that the Greeks and all ancient peoples used them. One can imagine that it would have been the sweet smelling leaves, flowers and seeds which were first found to have the greatest appeal, since their effect is immediate. Gardens in ancient Greece were planted with fragrant herbs and so were graves, which often formed a part of a garden. Even so, many of the

esteemed plants were gathered from the countryside. Gradually, for convenience, some of these were brought into the gardens and cultivated. Here they would be at hand when required. Many were imported from one country to another.

As they grew in importance and as time went by the knowledge of certain plants and their virtues passed, as was natural, into the hands of those who could write and teach. And so, as the centuries pass, we find that after the ancient civilizations it is the monks who are the most informed. A garden proper was an essential part of monastic life. After all, sufficient vegetables, enough to form the bulk of the daily food, had to be cultivated. And as such establishments had to be as self-supporting as possible, all herbs, medicinal and culinary, had also to be grown along with flowers for the church.

Monks in one country had contact with religious houses in others. People, treasures and plants were constantly being exchanged. Highly placed priests accustomed to equally high living insisted that the food they were about to enjoy in a foreign country should be as savoury as the dishes they had left behind them. And so far as healing plants were concerned we can be sure that not only fresh, growing plants were exchanged, but precious packets of certain proved and efficacious dried herbs as well. In time, those herbs used in cooking in one country would be sent or brought to the other.

One should not conclude that such gardens would be dull and flowerless. Lilies, paeonies, poppies, roses and violets and other flowers had both medicinal and religious value and would be grown for both reasons. Their

beauty would be a mere incidental bonus. Violets were 'herbs well cowth' and were eaten as salads, particularly with onions and lettuce. With fennel and savory they featured among the ingredients for a broth. Hawthorn, primroses and roses were also cooked.

A 'noble garden'

In the 12th Century the Abbot of the Augustines at Cirencester wrote a great poem in 10 parts. In the 7th book he praised the excellence of such herbs as betony, centaury, plantain and wormwood. In another of his works, *De Naturis Rerum*, he described a noble garden. It 'should be adorned with roses and lilies, turnsole, violets and mandrake; there you should have parsley and cost, and fennel and southernwood and coriander, sage, savory, hyssop, mint, rue, dittany, smallage, pellitory, lettuce, garden cress, paeonies. There should be planted beds with onions, leeks, garlick, pumpkins and shalots, cucumber, poppy, daffodils and acanthus should be in a good garden. There should also be pottage herbs such as beets, herb mercury, orach, sorrel and mallows.'

Marsh Mallow, *Althea officinalis*, was included in most physic gardens. Its starchy roots were used in poultices, ointments and sweetmeats, hence 'marsh mallows', a favourite sweetmeat for centuries.

In a description of a Saxon monastic garden one reads of the 'hortus', a rectangular enclosure with a central path leading from the gardener's house and shed where the tools were kept, and also of the 'herbaularis', the smaller physic garden with a border of plants all around the wall, and four beds on each side of the

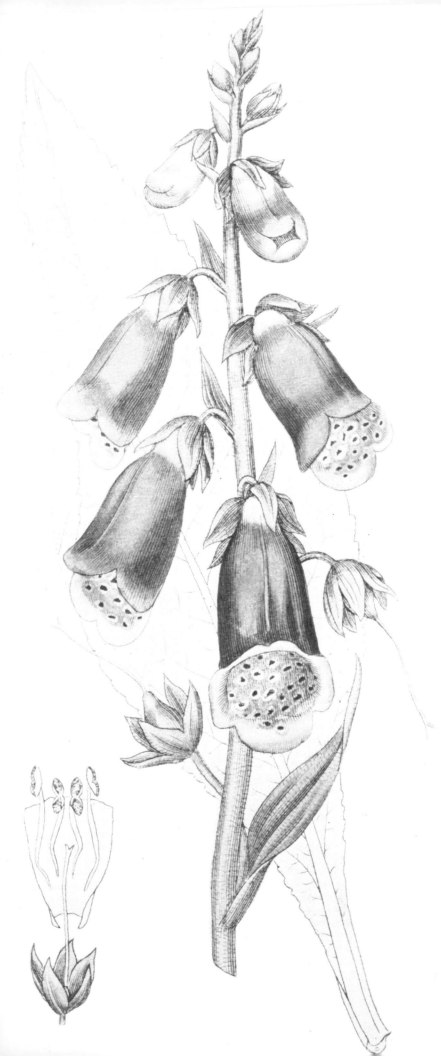

central walk. The plants growing in these beds were precisely labelled. Among a few of the Saxon names of herbs which can be traced to the Latin are coriander, chervil, cummin, feverfew, fennel, lovage, mint, poppy, parsley, rue and mustard.

By the Middle Ages we find that the ladies of the castles are the gardeners. They had been taught by the monks to cultivate healing herbs among their vegetables and culinary plants. And since these ladies also tended the sick, wounded and poor in both castle and village, this meant that the materials for such charities were always near at hand. The lady remained the gardener for centuries. When Erasmus wrote of gardens in the early 16th Century, he called the vegetable garden 'the Woman's Kingdom'. He suggested too that there should be a medicinal garden containing useful herbs for home use. Meanwhile, of course, culinary herbs were grown in quantity.

For the wealthy, meat and game were abundant. Vegetables would only be served in any quantity on fast days, but herbs were in demand for stuffings, flavourings and for sauces. This had been so for centuries.

We learn that all strongly flavoured herbs were popular in cooking. In the reign of Edward I fennel was in general use, both its leaves and its seeds, and obviously not only to flavour fish. As much as $8\frac{1}{2}$ lbs. of fennel seed was bought by the king's household for one month's supply, which might be compared with my own lavish, not to say reckless, 1 oz. for a year! Mint was also combined with it in sauces.

There is no doubt that strong herbs varied the dull winter diet

Purple foxglove, digitalis. Early herb books were real works of art as well as being minutely observed and illustrated scientific records of great value.

dicit̄ ꝓfecū

hō scordeon ten cū oleo laurino subacta dinorsas
ꝓ poste. Mōr collic. It̄ herba scordeon decocta ℥ cū
uel si denuraumo ponit. ipsa āu ūusta d isplaga
posita. dolorū collet. Alliga ꝑ
hemini cordianas t̄ ūnatus
t̄ collet.

nom̄ herbe unbarocum ·
Agrec̄ dr̄ slomon. Alū dr̄ ligmnos
ẽ ꝓtibꝭ ermorabidos. Egyptii dic̄ nachil ·
dacu uos dract̄ dr̄ t̄rale uerbascū.
Nascit̄ locis sablosis · t̄ huic herbā
mercuri inuenit. d ulyꝭ dedit cū
nouisse. Addract̄ · ut ē malasara
ū rimore. Aduersus occursus
malos ·ii· hō uerbascū uirgulā
ꝗ sacū ꝑmulte t̄ nullo modo tcrr̄dt.
neꝗ hostig neꝗ occurs mali illi
nocebit̄ Adpodagras ·iii·
hō uerbascū cū ūusta atꝗ
jpasm · dolorū auferre. d esficacū solut. ut abilare
Alis sidonius uocant. nom̄ herbe oradca. Laudaw ·
Alii scoparmion · Alii cornaton. Alii ordios dic̄. Alii atr̄
cas. Alii herculanea. Alii pariscū.
Alii seruraueane.
hō oradcū si uoru ꝑtuluit. Lauro
nes n̄ runobis. scsuagit cū eos. Adca
ligmō odōz ·ii· hō oradca gn̄a par

gal. c̃dc̃ habem caligine inmeat. Albuginé tollit · nom̄ herbe
celidonia ·
Alii dñt· Alii
rea· Alii melision·
egypan arbonea ·
alii mopop. leuli grindig̃
uocant· Romani celidonia dicũt.
Ad caligine et albuginé
et uulnera oculorũ · I·
her̄ celidonie succũ cũ sua radice
pibis cũ uino uci cũ melle uino
prrie albo · cũ muleb̃ bene erecú
fuerit· tunges et cure· caligine dis̄cret·
Ipsi oepin sunt· q̃dã de succo eñ· uli tacro
celossibi inungono · II· her̄ celidonie
succũ et flores cõuere· et exp̄ssos milcos
cũ melle attice · et tunges· et cupit
magnũ clarititem · nom̄ herbe strignos·

Adignõ
sacrum ·
Atrucuã supinam·
· I· her̄ strignos suũ terã
et supterrũ· ign̄ cã ereã mirã
lice cure· Ad Alloprias · II·
her̄ strignos et eis suf mirtheo
curac alloprias · III· her̄ strignos
de aceto celefacris et fullera
mirtheo capris dolore tollit· Ad
dentiũ dolore· IIII her̄ strignos et matris
mirtheo sacrũ si dentes corat· Ad sanguiné si
de naribz effluit· v· her̄ strignos süc̃ clara uineo·
et aribz imittis· sanguiné mirtheo filugro·

of tough meat, pickled and salted yet flavourless. And as so many herbs were believed to have prophylactic virtues, in summer these would be used to still queasy stomachs and to take the edge off the uninviting pungency of any meat that had been kept too long. At the same time they would also help to flavour meat which had to be eaten freshly killed, because it would not be safe to hang it during hot, fly-infested days.

In old books, histories, plays and stories we get glimpses of what herbs were most favoured and sometimes why they were in demand. In *Piers Ploughman* a priest asks of a poor woman: 'Hast thou ought in they purs? Any hot spices?' and she answers, 'I have peper and piones (paeonies) and a pound garlike, A ferthyng-worth of fenel seed for fasting days.'

And in Chaucer's *Romaunt of the Rose*:

'Then went I forth on my right
   hond,
Downe by a litel path I found
Of Mintes full and Fennell
   greene.'

It was the purely useful plants that were first given garden room. We have to remember that the cultivation of plants for the sake of their medicinal and culinary virtues went hand in hand with people's delight in the fragrance of their flowers and leaves.

The flower garden was derived from the herbal garden. It was not until late in the Renaissance that it developed parallel to it. Long before this educated people interested themselves in botany and for this the impetus came from the ever-growing imports of foreign plants from countries which were being opened up to explorers. 'Many foreign healing plants have been naturalised with us, rare and remarkable in their useful properties and hitherto unknown to us who own land', wrote Olivier de Serres in about 1600. In Italy public botanic gardens were first established. Even where private gardens also reaped a benefit from the imports, the herbs were still set apart. There were gardens within gardens, places set aside for certain kinds of plants.

In a later edition of Holinshed's *Chronicle* of 1587 we read of herbs, plants and fruits which were being brought in every day from India, America, the Canary Islands and all parts of the world. Following Italy's example special botanic gardens were established in England where foreign medicinal herbs were cultivated. John Gerard had a famous scientific garden in Holborn at the end of the 16th Century.

Both father and son Tradescant, gardeners to Charles I, made a collection of plants which was to form the basis of the Ashmolean Museum. In their time, in the king's garden, by the year 1648, some 1600 plants were grown in one part alone.

Even as early as Tudor times a physic garden was an essential:

'Good Aqua Composita, vinegar
   tart,
Rose water and treakle to
   comfort the hart.
Cold herbs in hir garden for
   agues that burn
That ouer strong heat to good
   temper may turn.

Get water of Fumentorie,
   Liuer to coole
And others the like, or else lie
   like a foole
Conserue of the Barberie,
   Quinces and such
With sirops that easeth the
   sickly so much.'

The still room where herbs were dried, pounded and distilled, where conserves, flowers and sweet waters, pot-pourris and most other 'necessities' were made, was and remained until quite recent times an important part of a well run household. Gifts of distilled herbs were often exchanged and were treasured. These were things readily accepted by the wealthy from their poorer friends. Today one wonders for what purpose the many distillations were used, for the liquids obtained were essences rather than spirits.

The Household Book of the 5th Earl of Northumberland, 1502, contains a list of herbs 'to stylle'. It includes 'borage, columbine, buglos, sirrel, cowsloppes, scabious, wild tansy, wormwood, endyff, sauge, dandelion and hart's tongue'.

Meanwhile, and aided by many books on the subject, men interested themselves in designing gardens all the better to display the plants or exploit them in some way. At Hampton Court, rosemary was 'so planted and nailed to the walls as to cover them entirely'.

Sweet smelling

Bacon describes walks which were planted with sweet smelling herbs. 'Those which prefume the air most delightfully, not passed by as the rest, but being trodden upon and crushed, are three – that is, burnet, wild thyme and water-mints: therefore you are to set whole alleys of them to have the pleasure when you walk or tread.'

Camomile was used (and still is) in this manner. In Shakespeare's *Henry IV*, Act 2, Scene 4, Falstaff says, 'For though camomile, the more it is trodden on the faster it grows; yet youth the more it is wasted, the sooner it wears'.

Overleaf: Two pages from a 12th Century English Herbal.

The quantity of medicinal and magic plants grew in numbers and variety, but gradually the old superstitions which related to the powers of certain plants began to wane. Many of these were exposed and ridiculed during the Commonwealth, for such beliefs were anti-puritan. However, in some country districts some belief lingered on, and indeed is still to be found in certain parts.

Early traders

The vast increase in foreign trade led not only to imports into Europe of herbs and spices, but also exports to trading posts and settlements abroad. Early traders in America, for example, were soon sending to Europe such widely separated exotics as chilli peppers and vanilla pods and before long courtiers in a French castle and puritans in Pennsylvania were both using an international 'manufactured' flavouring made up in part from Mexican chillis, Egyptian cumin and Chinese ginger. But only the simplest and most necessary of herbs were actually grown in domestic gardens on both sides of the Atlantic. Records exist of gardens in Salem, Plymouth, Charlestown, dating back to 1682, indicating that in private gardens the emphasis was on plants for food – cabbages, beans and corn – with herbs such as rosemary, pennyroyal and coriander grown from European seed.

Meanwhile in Europe the import of plants, particularly the truly medicinal plants, gradually influenced the very shapes and designs as well as the contents of gardens, and gardening was a pursuit for both the wealthy and the scholarly.

When King Charles V of Spain, a keen botanist, retired into a

This illustration from an early book of herbs is of Common henbane, Hyoscyamus niger. *Look at the careful detail in the seed and flower.*

13

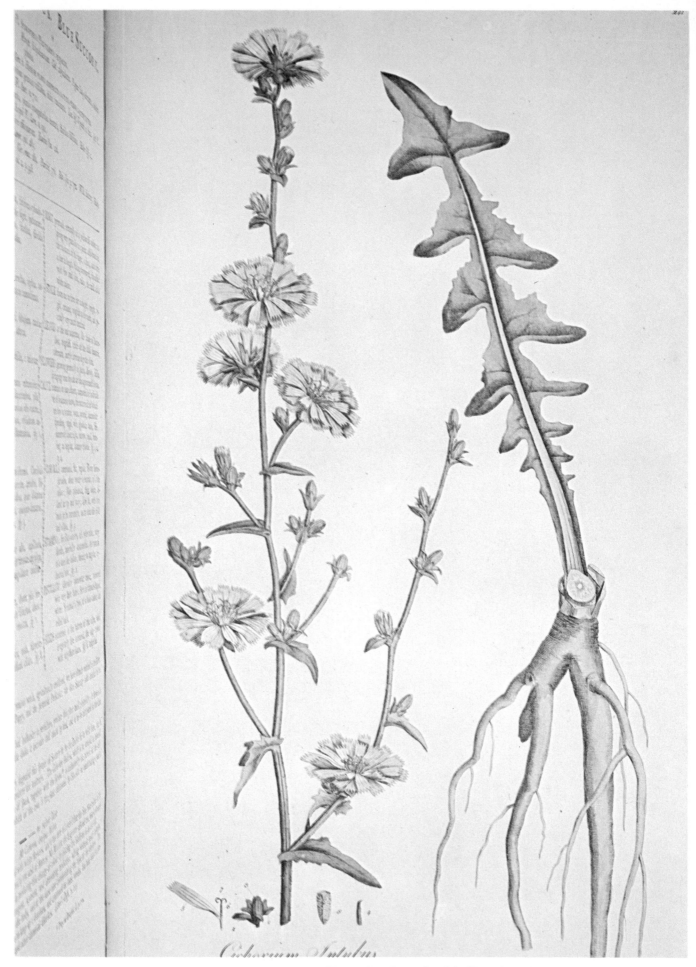

Chicory, Cichorium intybus, *an illustration from Curtis's* Flora Londinensis.

Betony, Betonica officinalis, *also from Curtis's* Flora Londinensis. 15

monastery of San Jeronimo at San Juste, he built a house and made a garden on the terrace on which grew citrus fruits and sweet scented herbs. To this place from every part of Spain's great empire overseas came new plants from the distinguished botanists and plant hunters of the day.

More and more books came to be written and more and more gardens were laid out. In 1600, Olivier de Serres, writing in *Le Theatre d'Agriculture*, advised that the garden be divided into departments for kitchen products, flowers, medicinal herbs and fruit trees and vineyards. In discussing the flower garden or bouquetier, he suggested that parterres be filled with flowers and various plants and that for edges of the parterre, the gardener must use sweet scented low growing plants such as lavender, thyme, mint, marjoram and many others. These remained fashionable in many gardens, and we can have no doubt that where these had to be clipped to keep them low and neat the clippings would be used fresh or dried or even distilled. However, by the 1700's the slower growing box was superseding these plants as an edging.

This really is worthy of comment, for box trees are said to smell of foxes. Few people, if any, found the scent of the plant pleasing. It seems that for the first time in gardening convenience overtook the delights of the senses.

One wonders whether this might not have been seen as a portent, as a sign of the times to come, when so much that entailed long hours of labour would be thrust aside, and perhaps lost for ever. Where now, for instance, are the still rooms, or more pertinently, where are those who could work in them

for so long for such little reward? Yet the many things that were made in them could bring us delight and solace today. It seems that yesterday's labour could well – and with great benefits other than financial – become today's hobby.

The study of the history and the universal use of herbs and medicinal plants in general could easily become a life's work. Here I can hope to do no more than sketch briefly some of the influences which were responsible for the great interest in these plants which persisted for centuries. And I can only ponder and reflect upon the decline in that interest. No doubt many modern factors came to bear, mainly at the same time. Not least significant are the advances in medicine as well as the growing confidence of the public in their doctors and in the efficacy of modern drugs. One feels that there must have been a great deal of hit and miss about plant medicines!

Coupled with the advances in medicine there is also the gradual elimination of dire poverty in many parts of the world and the introduction of health services so that fewer people have to try to heal or cure themselves. Modern sanitation, sewage systems, cleaner bodies, all of these things have had an influence on the plants we grow and the disappearance of some from the garden scene. Naturally, culinary herbs, with their close associations with vegetable growing, would be the last to be influenced and in fact most of these never disappeared entirely.

The gradual movement of people from the countryside to industrial areas meant a decline in the knowledge of native plants and herbs and fewer people to gather

them, less space in the garden, less time to cultivate them, less time to conserve them. Factory-made sauces and catchups were more convenient and in time these took pride of place on the table in millions of homes. Dried herbs also became a factory product. A few years ago even the demand for packeted dried herbs declined. Now it is rising again every year and those who found their way to the use of herbs through packeted, dried kinds are seeking information on fresh kinds. More and more people want to grow them.

A decline

Even with the foregoing explanation it is still surprising that herbs went through such a decline in some countries. One great factor, I believe, is the woman in the garden. As we have seen, for centuries this was her domain. At what point, one wonders, was it no longer her prerogative to plant the vegetable plot, to supervise how the family's food should be grown, even to tend the vegetables herself? For it is certainly the case that in recent years home gardeners, generally speaking, divide the garden into his and hers; she looks after the flowers and he the vegetables. Obviously there must be a degree of co-operation, but in the vegetable garden at the moment the man rules supreme. Perhaps horticultural shows helped in the decline of herbs. After all, a humble bunch of thyme is not such a fit object for admiration as a giant leek, onion or parsnip. However, seedsmen tell me that this scene also is changing. More and more women are cultivating vegetables, and more and more are growing unusual kinds, and with these, a great variety of fresh herbs. Today herbs of all kinds are finding a place in the ornamental garden as well as in the kitchen plot. So many also have proved themselves to be excellent patio, balcony, and even roof garden plants. No wonder they are popular. Few plants are decorative and utilitarian as these are.

Herbs are demure plants. They hide their qualities as they do their savours. Only when you cultivate them, when you get to know them really well, do you discover these.

Today we need herbs. Mass produced foods tend to pall, but they can be made interesting, even memorable, by the discreet and intelligent addition of herbs. Frozen food often suffers from being so fresh that it does not taste as it should. The right herb can play on the taste, bring it out, improve the dish. Food is becoming more and more expensive as it so rightly finds its way onto tables or into bowls which tended so often to be empty. Herbs can give the simplest of foods, pasta, eggs, bread, rice, a variety of flavours so that these can be served time and time again in so many ways that one never tires of them.

As I said earlier, at one time gifts of sweet waters, pot-pourris, sachets, lavender bags and many other perfumed trifles exchanged hands. These were something the not so rich could give to the wealthy. And the same holds true today. If you are a giver and if you have a herb garden you have a great store of riches. You have within your reach many gifts that money cannot buy. All you have to give is a little talent and time, time to grow, time to gather, time to present herbs in any way that you fancy. If you live a busy life you need not find this demanding. And the wonderful thing is that as you make a gift you give yourself one as well, for to work with herbs is to savour a very pleasant facet of life. Your gifts will have a quality which cannot be marketed, for with each will go not only a tiny fragment of your garden but also of your life and you.

Meanwhile you can bring a touch of delight to your garden by planting herbs. Even when my own large garden is full of colour from other plants, I notice that my guests all linger by the herb bank, bruising this plant, fondling that one, savouring the scents from the varied leaves in greys, greens, bronzes and many variegations. Here, it seems, is the heart of the place and I think that every garden should have a heart, just as every dish should have its own special herb associated with it.

This illustration of the elaborate flowers of Viper's bugloss, or Echium plantagineum, *is taken from Sowerby's magnificent book of* English Botany.

17

Herbs in the Modern Garden

When we consider that gardens were originally created to grow herbs, to have them near at hand when needed, it seems strange that many people are now inclined to regard these plants as something quite distinct, even a little odd. Herbs are often found tucked away in a special herb garden or plot and, although some of these separate gardens do have a charm of their own, it should be kept in mind that most herbs can be grown among other plants in the garden and thus form a part of the whole. This is especially the case for tiny gardens where there may not be sufficient space to create a herb plot apart from the remainder.

Some herbs, like lavender and rosemary, can make neat hedges and boundary borders. Others such as thymes, will cover the ground, even paving it with a fragrant, evergreen carpet. Camomile and pennyroyal can be used either with grass or without, as lawn plants. The tough, 'garden party' lawn at Buckingham Palace is of grass and camomile growing together. Mints will cover a bank and usefully anchor the soil. Angelica will bring architectural

Left: Herbs and flowers mixed together make a colourful border for every kind of garden. The mixed border in this picture looks very good.

Above: This low hedge of cotton lavender, Santolina makes a satisfying border to a flagstone path. Roses planted alongside add brightness to the main entrance.

beauty to a shady area. The lovely glaucous leaves of rue will shine throughout the winter, and during the winter it is useful for cutting for flower decoration, as are many other herbs. Purple sage will make a splendid bush. Borage flowers have a wonderful blue quality.

Naturally, the way you plant herbs will depend on how much garden room you have. If you have not yet introduced these plants, consider making a feature of them.

If you enjoy the form, textures and subtle hues of plants, and find in them better garden value than seed-packet riots of colour, bear in mind that herbs can make a lovely garden border. They do not have to be set into formal patterns. In such a border (possibly an island type, which can be walked around and admired on all sides) those plants with silver foliage, such as the curry plant, santolina, artemisias, lavenders and rue, can act as focal points or else be used to separate the mass of plants from the green lawn around them. There are many variations of hue, including variegated forms of common herbs, thymes and mints. Variegated balm has yellow splashes on its fine green leaves, as bright as lemons. Golden marjoram is highly prized as a garden plant even among those who are not looking especially for herbs. *Salvia officinalis* has given rise to many varieties. I grow the variegated *S.o. crispa* and the purple sage, *S.o. purpurascens*. To quote from the Royal Horticultural Society Dictionary of Gardening, 'The purple-leaved and variegated forms are useful in the pleasure garden, the purple-leaved form is one of the best evergreen plants of its colour and height,' a sentiment with which I entirely agree. All can be used in cooking, just like

the penny-plain types:

If, however, you like to see bright floral colours about your garden and find most herbs dull, the herb garden can be made bright. Old fashioned roses can be used as a background; dwarf, clipped lavender hedges can be of alternated plants, purple, pink, white and lavender; poppies and marigolds will seed themselves and flower each year among the perennials. If we accept, as I think we should, the bright nasturtiums as herbs, their vivid splashes of colour can be used to complement the lovely blue of borage. And in their seasons many of the herbs themselves will bloom. Few plants are prettier than a row of chives in flower, and the honey-filled florets can also be used in salads.

Herb bank

It is important to plant herbs where they will grow best. Like all other garden plants they include annuals, biennials and perennials, shrubs and, in the case of the sweet bay, a tree. Most of them like a well drained soil which does not need to be rich though it should be light – heavy soil affects the pungency of some herbs. My herb bank designed to screen and divide the kitchen garden from the remainder and to act as a wall against the north winds, is on the site of an old hedgerow, grubbed out and burnt. The bank has been built on this cleaned and burned ground from piles of soil excavated from other parts of the garden, heaps of lawn mowings, leaf sweepings, annual weeds and bonfire ash, topped with good loam made from rotted turves. It is nicely alkaline, and both light and well drained. One side faces south and on the other,

The illustration shows one possible layout for a herb corner in your garden. Behind the seat is bay. Pinks are in the two tubs; lavender in the right foreground.

Behind the sundial is a shrub rose, and immediately to the right a rosemary hedge. Around the base of the sundial are thyme, with the white flower, and parsley.

which faces north, there is shade for most of the day. This choice of aspects suits all types of herbs.

Exceptions to herbs growing best in light soil are the mints, which prefer heavier soil in light shade, although they will grow less luxuriantly in other places. Parsley and chervil are said to prefer moist but fertile soil, yet wherever my own plants seed themselves they grow mainly on the sunny side of my herb bank and not in the shade.

Good colour

Many of the herbs, especially the labiates, are shrubs, even though some, such as the thymes, are not very tall. If you have a mixed shrub border and little space to spare you can plant this type of herb in with the other shrubs, near the front so that you can get at them easily and because of their size. Fortunately they can all be clipped to keep them under control, although you are likely to find that picking them regularly keeps them trim enough.

Alternatively, you can plant herbs in a mixed border along with favourite shrubs and herbaceous plants. Many of them will give you good colour in the summer. There are, for instance, many lovely marjorams. Lavender blooms for several weeks and its soft grey foliage is decorative throughout the year. Rosemary blooms in spring and a well grown plant will become smothered in sweet blue-lipped flowers. Fennel can go to the back of the border where its fine yellow umbels can be seen silhouetted against the sky. Hyssop, pink and blue, will make good knots of colour. Chervil will follow the daffodils with a dainty Queen Anne's lace effect. Marjoram will attract the butterflies and smudge the border with soft rosy-purple clusters of flowers. It looks particularly striking with regale lilies.

Some herbs can be used as neat edgings in formal areas. Chives, cushiony thymes – both perennials – or biennial parsley can follow the edge of a path, where they are convenient for gathering. These look charming when alternated. Simply re-sow pinches of fresh parsley between the perennials each year.

A paved terrace, patio or path can be softly furnished by either creeping or sprawling herbs such as thyme or pennyroyal, growing in the spaces between the stones or perhaps in larger spaces specially left for them. Taller thymes can also be grown this way and as these will be kept regularly cut for cooking, the plants remain neat and cushion-like. Rosemary which sprawls engagingly, looks attractive and also smells good if it is planted near a stone seat. It also makes a good hedge.

Clipped bays

In a patio, a small paved garden or a backyard it is possible to use herbs exclusively and make a charming scene. Where there is a wall to be furnished the old Elizabethan practice of covering it with rosemary can be followed. Sturdy plants must be bought in the first place, of course. So long as the soil is suitable and the aspect favourable the stems will soon grow, but they must be trained from the beginning.

Clipped bays look well in these settings. However, bear in mind that these evergreens also make effective screens when left to grow naturally.

Three or more plants, mixed kinds preferably, will grow well in

*Left above: One of the many
thymes,* Thymus serpyllum, *grows
thickly and has a bright flower.
Left below: Pot marjoram,*
Origanum onites, *growing out-
of-doors.*

*Above: Golden marjoram, thyme,
curry plant, chervil and other
herbs planted closely together
make an attractive-looking corner
in any small garden.*

23

the space from which an average size paving stone has been lifted and removed. These will soften the harsh effect of paving, especially if they are allowed to sprawl in places. Golden marjoram looks particularly lovely. If you lift paving for a purpose such as this

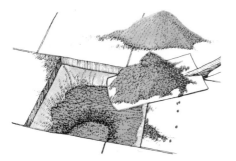

remember that the soil beneath will be out of condition, so it is always best to remove the first foot or so and replace it with fresh soil from another spot.

In a backyard, or in a town garden where the soil is old and spent, herbs will grow best on raised borders. These can be just one brick high, but made higher they ease the labour of gardening, particularly for the elderly. The area above ground level should be filled with imported soil, preferably rich and loamy. Once again rosemary can be grown against a wall. Tall lavenders can also be trained this way at the back of a narrow border – a good way to use them. Spreading plants can be encouraged to grow over the stone edges of the raised beds, and large ones such as angelica and the tall yellow-bloomed fennel can be given regal treatment, for they are strong enough to be made into special features. The bronze-leaved fennel is especially handsome. Bear in mind, though, that these are at their best in summer and site an evergreen or similar feature nearby so that there is some-

thing to admire in winter; a Provence pot containing growing herbs, a seat or even a statue perhaps. Alternatively, some plant skeletons can be both decorative and dramatic in winter, especially on the mornings when they become frosted, and I recommend that you let these remain.

Remember that angelica, as it is biennial, must be continually renewed. You will need to save some seed and keep a stock going.

If you are concerned about any of these plants becoming too tall, or especially in the case of fennel that the seedlings from the scattered seed stems will grow too readily to be really welcome, simply keep the flower stems cut and thus reduce both the height and the fecundity of the plants. If you hope to save the fennel seed, and harvest it at the proper time, you should have no problem.

If you feel that it is best for your purpose to set aside a separate plot, see if there is a sunny, sheltered area near the kitchen door so that you haven't far to go on wet days, and should you wish to gather herbs after dark locate your herb patch where a shaft of light from a doorway or window will show you what plants you want to gather. It may even be worth your while to install a special light for this purpose.

Steady supply

A small patch of earth, even just a yard by about four feet, is large enough to provide a steady supply of essential herbs such as parsley, thyme, sage, mint and chives. This can be extended by using contained herbs near the house (see the next chapter). A bay tree in a tub looks well at the side of a door and a pair look even better. Clipped rosemary and sev-

eral other herbs can be grown the same way.

Herbs which are to be used in quantity are usually best grown in rows, either along a path behind a border or across a kitchen garden plot. If you wish to confine them to one area it is best to group the

various kinds. Plants suitable for rows are parsley – including the less curly-leaved Hamburgh parsley which is grown for its roots as well as its tops – chervil, chives, shallots and garlic. But I must stress that any of these can be grown in groups instead and are,

of course, just as effective.

Some herbs are best grown from seed and all good seedsmen stock them, or at least some of them. Although you get good value for money from seed, in some cases it may not be practical to raise plants in this way. You may find

it economical in the long run to buy mature plants, even if each costs more than a packet of seed. Some **must** be grown from seed I would say. These are the annuals and some biennials. They include anise, basil, borage, caraway, chervil, coriander, cumin, dill, parsley, summer savory and sweet marjoram. Not all annuals will transplant well and so it is usual to sow these thinly where they are to mature and to thin them out gradually as they grow, each time removing the weakest plants and making more room for those which are growing strongest. However, if the seedlings are raised in peat pots and can be planted without disturbing their roots, they can be transplanted. Summer savory, marjoram and basil are often grown this way.

Mild winter

You can ensure supplies of fresh herbs in winter by lifting certain plants in autumn, or at any time during a mild winter, and bringing them into the greenhouse or even the house to force them into early growth. The types which can be treated thus are described in the chapter on Herb Families.

Most herbs are sun lovers and originate from warm regions, though few are tropical. If your garden is on heavy soil always plant and divide the herbs in spring. When you plant them sit each mass of roots on a bed of clean sand to ensure good drainage, after first forking over the bottom of the planting hole to aerate the lower soil. When you have finished planting spread a little more soil near the crown of each herb and give it a little collar of peat mulch to deter slugs and to lighten the soil texture.

Giant fennel, Foeniculum officinalis, *grows strongly in the summer. It can be used decoratively in flower arrangements, as well as for cooking.*

Herbs in Containers

The handsome sweet bay growing in a smart tub must surely be the classic example of a herb as a contained plant, and I am sure that someone who is no gardener may think that the plant is never grown in any other way than confined and carefully groomed. Yet bays will grow high, wide and handsome.

This is the only tree among the herbs, and it is interesting that we see it confined more than any other. You might think that the tree could be the most difficult type of herb to grow in a container. It has, in fact, proved to be the most popular. It is so attractive when grown in this way that it is often chosen for its appearance and not for its use.

This method of growing a bay is international. Surely this should encourage us to try growing other herbs in the same way? If it is possible to grow a tree in a pot we should be able to grow the shrubby kinds equally well, and if these will grow then surely the herbaceous kinds will tolerate confinement also? And indeed this is so.

For some years I grew many

Left: Chives, Allium schoenoprasum, *make a cheerful addition to a window box or grow just as well in pots by themselves.*

The sweet bay, Laurus nobilis, *is the only tree among the herbs, and has always been very popular for growing in tubs and large pots.*

27

herbs in containers high on a roof in the centre of the city, and in these exceptional conditions I learnt a great deal about these plants. I found for instance that mint, which is said to prefer a moist soil in a shady spot in a garden, would grow quite well in light soil in a pot. Actually I raised good crops in pots and boxes, although these had to be watered constantly during hot and dry spells – and it can get very hot indeed in a roof garden. Mint certainly grew lusher in the few pots that stood in the shade, but I proved that you can grow mint in a pot in a hot situation. However, fail to water it properly and you can expect trouble, as a rule in the shape of red spider.

Parsley is also said to prefer moist yet fertile soil, but again I planted parsley in the stone trough on the lower roof, where it confounded all the experts. It grew, flourished, flowered, dropped seed and reproduced itself vigorously in soil which was constantly drying out and in a place which was windswept and sun-baked.

One would expect thyme to enjoy a baking since we so often find it growing wild on some exposed and sunny bank. This also grew well up in the sky, and flowered prettily. Even bees, in the heart of the city, found it when it bloomed. Fennel, sage, chives and lavender were other roof garden tenants. These were grown in large containers or in raised beds around the perimeter of the flat roof.

Having begun so well, and so high, I have since had no qualms about growing herbs in containers at ground level. They can look most attractive, and now that there are so many plant contain-

Provence pots, smart white black-banded tubs, urns and big flower pots all have their places in patios, courtyards and paved areas.

28

ers from which to choose, contained herbs can be designed to suit any setting. Provence pots on paved areas, smart white black-banded tubs in a cottage courtyard, stone, plastic, fibreglass, concrete troughs, bowls, saucers – all have their part to play. Any good garden container will do. In one farmhouse I visited all the herbs were grown outside the kitchen in great stone drinking troughs, warm with the sun in summer and so thick that they protected the roots in winter.

Visual effects

Let us begin in the place most dedicated to the contained garden, the outside window-sill. Here a window-box can become a prolific little herb garden, sufficient to supply the small family with a succession of fresh herbs. But it needs to be well designed. By this I mean that plants likely to grow large, sage, rosemary and tarragon for instance, are best planted at the side of the box and the centre kept for the smaller plants which are not likely to block out so much light from the room behind.

The box itself must be deep enough to hold enough soil for plants which are to grow lush and will be cut frequently. It should never be less than six inches. Obviously you should also be concerned with visual effects and a very deep box can be ugly, so try to strike the happy medium.

It is best to decide which herbs you most often use and see if these will be suitable to grow outside your window before you begin planting. Fennel, for instance, would not do, for its roots grow too deep and its stem too tall (although it will grow in any deep container) but basil, chives, thyme, parsley, sage, marjoram,

savory and tarragon (which grows tall but is kept short by cutting) will all do well. If you use a lot of chives, plant a row of these along the front of the box and cut alternate plants to keep them uniform and looking as attractive as possible. Sage likes a really deep container so if your window-box is shallow find a separate pot or tub for it.

If you want to include mint I suggest that you make a special division for it, so that although it is in the herb community it is in fact planted separately. This way you isolate its roots which are inclined to wander and become invasive. The same thing goes for balm. A tile slipped down inside the box fitting across it closely will do for this. Alternatively, slip the mint roots inside a plastic bag or the bag type of plastic pot. In the garden, some people plant mint in a bottomless bucket to keep its wandering roots under control yet providing means for the moisture to rise from the soil. A bag or pot does the same in a window-box.

You can also have a window-

*Slip mint roots inside
a plastic bag to isolate
the roots from other plants
in the tub.*

box inside your kitchen and the plants will thrive there so long as the light is good and there are no domestic gas or oil fumes in the atmosphere. Unlike plants in the open air those grown indoors are apt to become drawn, and generally speaking they are not so long-lived. It is best if you arrange the box so that it can be turned constantly thus giving all the plants a spell in full light. This way growth will be more even and the plants less drawn. Many of the plastic plant troughs on sale are light to handle and are quite suitable for herbs.

Best method

A great deal depends on how green-fingered you are and how good is the soil in which the herbs are planted. Apart from window-boxes some herbs grow well indoors. Rosemary, for example, will grow very well throughout the winter and can be stood outside still in its pot in summer. If potted herbs are really your best means of indoor herb gardening and if you have space outside to stand them, the best method is to have a number of herbs of the same kind growing at one time. These can be brought in and exchanged for plants which have become spent. Three plants is a good number: one in use, a new one at hand and one recovering. Most herbs can be grown this way and if you do not have a garden or a large plot it is a good way to ensure a regular supply. However, it is dependent upon having a standing ground for the pots not in use indoors, and people living in flats might find this method impractical unless the outside window-sills, a balcony or a small roof space can be used. If you are a gardener you would be doing a great service by

providing a friend with ready planted pots of this kind and taking the spent pots back home to recover.

Chives are ideal plants for pot culture. Those who have no gardens will probably find it simplest to raise a fresh crop from seed each year. In the garden chives should be lifted and divided every three or four years, a practice which ensures that the gardener gets many surplus plants – enough for him to fill pots for friends, as well as providing him with a supply to force early in the season.

Mint grown in a pot on the window-sill is best kept standing in a saucer of water. First make sure that when you prepare the pot for planting you fill the lower third of its depth with drainage materials such as broken flower pots, crocks, brick, shingle, pebbles or small stones, even nuggets of non-water-retentive plastic, all mixed liberally with charcoal nuggets. The charcoal you buy for barbecues is splendid and very cheap. By doing this the soil keeps moist, yet because of the drainage layer it is also well aerated.

You can grow mint in a glass jar as you would a hyacinth bulb, and it will also grow in a puddle pot, that is in pebbles and water and sustained by small but regular doses of soluble plant food. In each case be sure to use some charcoal to keep the water sweet.

Many plants can be lifted in the autumn and grown on indoors, either in the home or under glass. Parsley is usually treated this way and you can also over-winter fennel, tarragon and basil. If you would like to use fresh herbs throughout winter rather than dried ones, lift and pot some and at the same time protect some

There are so many varieties of mint and they are all ideal for a scented garden. Right above: Mentha pulegium, or pennyroyal, is also decorative when it flowers

thickly. Mentha gentilis, var. gracilis, in the near right picture, has larger leaves and is more commonly used for cooking.

Far right: Champion moss curled parsley, Petroselinum crispum, is one of many herbs that you can bring indoors during the winter to have fresh and to hand.

more of the same kind by covering them with cloches.

On my own kitchen window-sill as I write is a terracotta crocus pot, the kind with pocket holes made at intervals all over its circular sides, each intended to hold a crocus bulb. In spring the pot is then a mass of flowers. Instead of bulbs my pot contains herbs. There are chives in the top and rings of parsley, thyme and sweet marjoram. The seed of all but the parsley, seedlings of which were lifted from the garden, were sown in early spring and raised on the window-sill. As soon as they were large enough to handle safely they were pricked off into the crocus pot, one seedling to each hole. The parsley seedlings would have grown indoors, but these need a longer period of germination and so should have been sown earlier than the others.

At the same time each day the pot is given a quarter turn so that each segment gets equal light and the growth of the herbs is kept as even as possible. By late spring some of the marjoram plants had grown so well that they needed pinching out and so I began using this particular herb from time to time even though the plants were so young. The shoots were nicely pungent. Once the growing point of the main stem had been nipped out the side stems began to grow well.

Also for kitchen windows are various kinds of hanging baskets or specially designed pots which can be suspended to save space and get good light. Parsley can be grown in the old fashioned type of wire hanging basket, or you can also use a salad drying basket. The plants are grown in the top of the baskets and the seedlings or small plants are also planted through the wires over the outer surface of the basket so that when they are fully grown you have a globe of green. The drawback to this type of container is that it must be well watered, and watering can be a messy, drippy business. A container which does not drip and which can be suspended is much more convenient. Other herbs than parsley can be grown this way, basil and knotted marjoram in particular.

Soluble food

My herbs are growing in one of the so-called soil-less composts. These are peat based and have the requisite plant foods incorporated. After about two months I shall begin feeding the plants with a soluble plant food for by this time most of the existing nutrients will have been used by the growing plants or leached from the soil.

If you want to grow herbs in any kind of container it is important that you begin with a good potting compost. Different types of these are on sale at all garden stores and centres. The soil-less types are light in weight, an important point for some people in certain conditions. However, where these lightweight composts are used out of doors, for instance in window-boxes or tubs where at first, while the plants are young, they do not cover the surface, I suggest that it is both wise and beneficial to cover the soil surface with a layer of clean horticultural sand or with washed shingle or some similar material. This will prevent the precious compost from being blown away on windy days or in windy places. It will also keep the roots cool by preventing too rapid moisture loss.

Two good ideas for growing herbs in containers. Right: A special earthenware herb-jar with chives at the top, then marjoram, parsley and, at the bottom, thyme.

Far right: A hanging basket overflowing with parsley. It not only looks good but is very handy for last minute additions to vegetable dishes or fish.

If you feed the plants from time to time (and when you do be sure to follow the directions very carefully and precisely) you can go on using the same compost for quite a long time for the same plants. It is a good plan to rejuvenate it each spring by giving it a fresh top dressing. Remove the top inch of soil and replace with fresh.

Tough, shrubby plants like rosemary originate in the hot, dry *garigue* areas of the Mediterranean and they can get by with little water, though it is surprising what a difference a plentiful supply makes to them. If you want a good supply of fresh, tender herbs you must be prepared to water lavishly those which are contained, especially if they are in very sunny, exposed places. It helps also to spray the foliage in the early morning before the sun hits it, and on summer evenings. Besides refreshing the plant and helping to keep it turgid this practice also keeps the leaves clean. Remember that the softer and lusher the nature of the leaves the more dependent is the herb on moisture. But be sure that you do not kill the plants by drowning, something much easier to do with plants growing indoors than those which are outside.

When potting soil composts are used it is necessary to place a really good layer of some kind of drainage material at the base of the container. It should fill at least a quarter of the vessel. This ensures that any surplus water that sinks is held in this open layer so that it does not make the soil waterlogged. The soil-less composts behave differently and it is not so important to provide a drainage level for them. All con-

tainers used outside should have drainage holes in them so that water can seep away. Indoors this is not so important and where there is no hole in the container one should provide a drainage level as for containers out of doors. Often a good layer of charcoal nuggets is sufficient.

Touch of style

If you have a paved area near your kitchen you could grow a great variety of herbs conveniently near to hand. These could be in tubs, either in the modern types or in those of more traditional styles according to the setting. It is not essential to reserve one container for one type of plant. I would suggest that if you mix them you choose one upright type such as sage, rosemary, lovage or tarragon; one sprawler such as marjoram, thyme, mint or savory; and one temporary

kind which can be raised from a pinch of seed sown among the perennials such as parsley, chervil or basil. Chives can go with any mixture.

On the other hand, and especially if you have a large patio, a few big isolated herbs could give it great style and atmosphere. For instance, giant angelica in tubs grouped in some shady spot have great beauty of form. Rosemary can be grown on a stem as a standard, like some picture book tree. These plants revel in the sun. They could tower over a mat of carpeting thyme planted below them. Lemon verbena, *Lippia citriodora*, is a splendid plant for a container in a protected area.

Main part

If the area in which you grow herbs is also the main part of your garden, remember that they can be alternated with showy

Above: A mixed tray of young plants. Make sure to give them plenty of water if they are in a sunny place.
Right: Rosemary, Rosmarinus pyramidalis, *does not need such constant watering.*

plants. Marigolds, borage, nasturtiums and poppies will all grow in containers. Some of the pot-pourri plants will grow this way also, particularly the scented leaved pelargoniums.

A word of caution: If you own a dog, raise the tubs on bricks if necessary so that the plants in them do not become soiled.

Small area

An attractive way of growing herbs in a small area and at the same time to restrict those with wandering roots is to make a three-tiered bed in much the same way as used for strawberries. Aluminium lawn edging would do for this, though if the bed could be made deeper the plants would do better. Bricks or concrete blocks can also be used and peat blocks too, so long as these are kept moist.

The lowest circle is left at, say, nine inches deep, then a smaller circle is placed on this in the centre and an even smaller circular bed on top of this. You can go higher, of course, if you wish, though by doing this you would tend to increase the shade on one part of the pyramid. Much depends on the style of the garden and the plants you wish to grow. Obviously those plants which thrive in dry conditions will go at the top, as well as those which are taller and upright growing. It is possible to make such a bed look quite attractive because little plants like thyme and summer marjoram can scramble prettily over the edges.

Touches of creative originality such as this do much to give a garden that individual and well loved look. They help you to establish your own personal stamp upon it.

1 *Nasturtiums* 2 *Pinks* 3 *Bergamot*
4 *Borage* 5 *Balm* 6 *Basil* 7 *Mint*
8 *Dill* 9 *Savory* 10 *Rosemary*
11 *Parsley* 12 *Chives* 13 *Sage*
14 *Lavender* 15 *Thyme* 16 *Pot*
Marigolds

Plants for Pot-Pourri

What is a pot-pourri? It is a mixture of dried flowers, leaves, roots and seeds, all of which are scented and will retain that same scent for a long period, at least a year, and according to what ingredients are used, usually much longer. In spite of its name, pot-pourri as such is not known in France, where the word means a mixture, a meat stew, a medley of songs or, literally, a rotten pot!

A 'mixture' is the operative word, for there are also certain flowers and leaves such as lavender which are dried and used alone, usually in sachets or sweet bags. It can be kept in a deep bowl (where it can be stirred and so refreshed from time to time) or in perforated containers to enable it best to scent the air of a room. It can be made up into sachets to be laid among linen or hung among clothes, or even pressed between books. Pot-pourris are not only for perfumery but can act as repellents to moths, fleas, bookworms and other pests. They can also be used for scenting bath water and for shampoos; rosemary is a fine shampoo herb and a good hair tonic.

At one time the usual basis

Left: *Pot-pourri — in France the words mean, literally, 'a meat stew' — but this picture shows the herbs and flowers that retain their scent the longest.*

Above: *A splendid selection of rambler and climbing roses in full and glorious bloom . . .*

for most pot-pourri mixtures was rose petals, but it is quite possible to make other mixtures according to what flowers and leaves are available.

Fixatives

To keep the fragrance strong for years one needs to include those constituents which are known as fixatives. The most important of these are dried and sliced, or more usually pounded or powdered roots, and they include calamus, a palm; khus-khus or *Andropogon squarrosus*, a fragrant grass whose other names include cus-cus, vetiver or vetivert, which has a sandal-wood-like fragrance when dried; orris or *Iris florentina*, which is scentless at first but which imparts a fragrance like violets as it ages; angelica and sweet cicely. People have been known to use talcum powder to replace pure orris root and as a substitute for some others. Citrus peels, thinly pared and powdered, are also good fixatives. Use an apple peeler to get really thin skins, dry slowly in a warm oven and then grind in an electric blender or coffee grinder.

Tangerine, lemon and orange peels are sweetest when dried. Gum benzoin and gum storax are also used. Gums are plant secretions. Gum benzoin comes from *Styrax benzoin*. Gum Olibanum is really a resin which is also called frankincense. There are many others, but the first two are more frequently used in pot-pourri.

If one or more fixatives are used the fragrance will be long lasting. Alcohol is also used in some recipes as are also certain essential oils. These are mainly used to establish a particular fragrance. Unfortunately these are so volatile that they soon lose their scent. They include oil of bergamot, musk and lavender among others.

Salt also appears to be a fixative and it figures importantly in many pot-pourri recipes. A writer in 1822 had this to say, 'Roses and other flowers whose fragrance only is wanted, and which is not injured by the flowers being bruised, are best preserved with salt. Roses, for example, if well rubbed or pounded with one-fourth their weight of common salt, and placed in a jar, will retain their odour for years. From such roses almost all the rose-water sold in shops is made; indeed we believe the water distilled from salted roses is even more fragrant, it will certainly keep better, than that which is distilled from the fresh-blown rose.'

Iodised salt is not suitable.

In some recipes, especially in old books, you may find references to 'balsam'. This is not likely to mean the plant of that name. Balsam is a fragrant mixture of an ethereal oil and a resin secretion found in hollow cavities or certain plant tissues.

The best known balsams are Balsam of Peru and Balsam of Tolu, taken from two trees of the pea family, *Toluifera pereirae* and *T. toluiferum*. Toluifera is the synonym of myroxylon, the name coming from myros (myrrh) and xylon (wood) which in this case is resinous and sweet scented. The balsam is collected from incisions made in the bark. It is instantly fragrant, 'warm' and lemony.

Other balsams are Balsam of Copaiba, from *Copaifera officinalis* and *C. lansdorffii*, both also of the pea family. Balsam of Tamacoari is from Caraipa or Moquilea species. Gurjum balsam is from *Dryobalanops aromatica*, the Sumatra or Barus camphor, much prized in the orient. Canadian balsam comes from the evergreen *Abies balsamea*. Where they cannot be prepared at home these oils and powdered roots can be bought or ordered from some chemists and herbalists.

In spite of the many other flowers and leaves which are used, to speak of pot-pourri is to think of roses and lavender, for these are the two with the most fragrant memories and which play the most important role in many mixtures. They are also splendid garden plants.

Sweet Solace
Lavender

Lavender, lavandula, from lavandus, to be washed. Lavender water was the sweet solace of the medieval sybarite, the soothing lotion in which those ague-heavy heads were bathed. The plant was then called llafant, and later lavyndul. The so-called 'English' lavender was esteemed mainly for its value in scenting bed linen. It was pressed between the layers lying in great linen chests. It was hawked around the streets in summer and anyone with the slightest aquaintance with the Cries of Old London will know that among them was the haunting call, 'Who will buy my sweet lavender?'

Lavandula officinalis, synonyms *L. spica* and *L. delphinensis*, is in the family labiateae, one of a genus of about 20 species of shrubs, sub-shrubs and perennial herbs. It comes from the Mediterranean region, the Canary islands and India. Because of this one would expect that in its hot home-

Right: Three different kinds of lavender. On the left, Lavendula spica; *at the top,* Lavendula nana autropurperea, *Hidcote purple; and bottom right,* Lavendula stoechas.

lands its scent would be most highly fragrant, being released by the sun. But apparently this is not so. It is sweeter-scented when grown in the colder, greyer lands. Three hundred acres of it were formerly grown near Mitcham, now a London suburb, and the oil of the lavender produced there realised six times the price of that distilled by the French growers. Even so, to grow well the plant likes a warm, dry, sunny position and it does best on a chalky soil. However, it will grow in any garden soil.

Nowadays we regard it as one of our most delightful decorative plants, but this was not always so. For centuries it was most valued as an edging and a hedge plant. Low edging plants were not allowed to flower, for if they did the compact growth would be lost. Dwarf forms have always been regarded with approval. You will find many of them in old gardens or in historical replicas of them.

There are several types of lavender including a white one. *L. spica gigantea* is the strongest growing form, *nana* is the dwarf and Munstead dwarf (named after the famous Gertrude Jekyll's garden) is a form of *nana* which has darker flowers and which blooms earlier. *L. nana alba* is white with silvery foliage. Loddon Pink has the palest pink flowers and soft silver leaves. There are also many varieties.

One used to see another listed, *L. vera*, but botanists do not now consider this to be a distinct species, merely a form of *spica*. This is the type known as Dutch lavender, said to be the strongest for oils for distillation. *Spica* is known as 'English' lavender. It is long lasting in more than one sense, for on the bush occasional flowers bloom until the winter.

Lavender grows from seed or cuttings. The latter are quite easy. They should be taken and struck in frames in late summer or in the open ground in a sheltered border in autumn. It is important to take old wood for cuttings. The older the wood the colder the treatment you should give. Handle the cuttings as little as possible. For instance, do not even trim the heel, simply push the cuttings firmly into the ground as quickly as possible.

If you want lavender only as a hedge and not as a flowering plant, you should clip it in spring, quite hard. But if you want a plant covered in flower, cut it after flowering: just tip the stems, that is, cut off the faded flower spike with just the two or three leaves below it.

Hedges which have become a little bare in places can be patched by layering stems from plants on either side of the gap.

Lavender wine

Lavender scented sugar was once much prized, no doubt in days before toothpaste. Flowers were pounded with three times their weight of sugar. This conserve would keep for a year. Lavender wine was made by taking a bottle of sack, adding three ounces of the lavender sugar candy and shaking often. It was then strained through a jelly bag and would be ready to drink after a week. In 1568 William Turner said that the flowers 'could be quilted in a cappe and daylye worne for all diseases of the head that come of a could cause'. He added that it 'comforts the brayne very well'.

If you wish to dry them or make lavender scent bottles from them, gather blossoms just before they come into bloom. If you wish to distil them take them a week later.

To make the 'bottles' take eleven fresh stems and a yard of narrow ribbon with a little extra to make a bow. Bunch the heads together. Tie them tightly under the flowers with the ribbon. Now bend back the stems so that they make a cage around the flowers. Take the long free end of ribbon, draw it through from the inside and keeping it quite flat weave it in and out, over and under the stems, drawing them close to the flowers. When the end is reached take a needle and cotton and stitch the end securing it firmly. Cover the stitching with a little bow.

Rosa, roses

For pot-pourri as well as for garden scent and atmosphere roses are very important. Buds, flowers and the foliage of certain kinds can be used. Any scented rose will make pot-pourri, but as you might expect, some varieties and species are better than others. Fragrant red petals, especially those of the old fashioned varieties, are the base of most good mixtures. *Rosa centifolia* was one of the roses from which the famous Attar of Roses was once made. *R. damascena*, the damask rose, is another. This wonderful rose, incidentally, is responsible for many lovely garden varieties and is also one of the parents of the Hybrid Perpetual roses.

R. eglanteria, the sweet briar, with exquisitely shaped buds, has fragrant foliage. It makes a good dwarf hedge which should be trimmed each spring to keep it in

Above: Lavender, Lavandula officinalis, *makes one of the most pleasing and traditional borders to a garden path. Right: Besides filling the garden with colour, roses are essential for pot-pourri.*

Here are three varieties, all very different — above left, 'Fantin Latour'; above right, Rosa centifolia; *below right, the beautiful 'Eden Rose'.*

good order. Remember to dry the clippings. Its synonym is *R. rubiginosa*.

Another with scented leaves and a foliage which appears almost to be varnished is the early flowering *R. primula*, the incense rose. The flowers are pale yellow and the bush is of upright growth.

R. gallica officinalis is *the* French rose, whose dried petals have for centuries been used for pot-pourri, for conserves and for sweetmeats of many kinds. It is the parent of many of the lovely old garden roses which have inherited the distinctive sweetness of its perfumed petals.

R. centifolia is the cabbage or Provence rose, with large, blowsy, double pink fragrant flowers. Its variety *muscosa* is the common moss rose whose buds are thickly 'mossed'. There are many varieties. *Rosa muscosa* 'William Lobb',

one of the many old roses in my own garden, has purple red buds opening to become flat roses with many blue-tinged purple petals.

The one drawback about these old roses is that they flower only once, unless you can count a second shy flowering sometimes in the autumn. I would not recommend them except where there is plenty of garden room to spare. On the other hand, fortunately they need little attention and can be left to grow naturally.

There are many modern roses with fragrant petals. These include mainly red roses such as Tallyho, carmine; Eden Rose, madder pink; Bacchus, cerise scarlet. Many of the modern types can also be grown as shrubs or as hedges.

Carnations and pinks

Next to roses come scented

pinks and carnations from the tribe dianthus, the divine flowers. The most strongly scented are the old fashioned, often blowsy, untidy kinds, with calyces which split and spill the petals instead of retaining them neatly cupped. These are not often on sale as cut blooms. The smart, sophisticated glasshouse varieties have tended to oust them, yet though they may be more smartly tailored they cannot surpass the old cottage varieties in scent.

Long ago they were called clove gilly flowers and were used, like rose petals, in many ways, in conserves, syrups and in vinegars, as prophylactics as well as pickles. The wine red petals were used to make mulled wine and to flavour wines. Thus the flowers were called 'sops' in wine. They were always included in mixed pot-pourris.

44   Rosa gallica officinalis   *Blanche Double de Coubert*

The annual marguerite carnations, though quite sweetly scented, are not so strongly perfumed as some of the old fashioned 'border' varieties. If you want to grow these flowers for pot-pourris it is best to search for, even beg for, just one or two plants of the strongest scented perennial varieties and to increase them rather than try to grow a great variety. In any case the plants need to be renewed and propagated frequently. The best way to do this is to layer the side shoots as soon as the plants have finished flowering.

Pinks may prove more productive. There are annual, biennial and perennial kinds, all mat-forming plants with flowers which have generally shorter stems than carnations. Those with the most petals are naturally of greatest value for the pot-pourri

maker. The double white Mrs Sinkins, which dates from the 18th century, is a beauty for this purpose. There is another lovely white variety, White Ladies. Pink Mrs Sinkins is a sport from Mrs Sinkins and is also very fragrant. Dusky, a double pink, has the old clove scent. May is a modern, Alwoodii a scented, variety.

These plants will all grow in ordinary but rich soil and they like the sun.

Any sweetly scented flower which will dry and retain its perfume can be used in a pot-pourri, and this means that it is much easier to make than it was in the days when it had some real importance in the home, for today some of the difficult-to-obtain oils and fixatives are less necessary simply because the range of perfumed flowers easily available to us is very much greater than in

years past. Some flowers that are not highly scented are sometimes used to provide colour – delphiniums for instance. It is even possible to buy a proprietary powder which will impart a fragrance to any dried petals whether or not these are naturally scented. This powder provides a quick and foolproof method of making pot-pourri, but it does mean that the petal mixtures all smell much the same.

Some flowers which can be used are listed here.

Alecost, *Chrysanthemum balsamita*. Tiny yellow buttons which add a little colour as well as a faint spicy perfume. Leaves may also be used.

Bergamot, *Monarda didyma*. The lipped flowers provide a pleasant dusky rose colour. They are not quite so well scented as the leaves which are very useful.

Border carnations

Mrs Sinkin's pinks

45

Borage, *Borago officinalis.* The flowers have no fragrance value but they are attractive in mixtures which tend to be dull. If the flowers are to be dried gather them just before they open.

Camomile, *Anthemis nobilis.* The creamy white daisies look charming in petal mixtures. If the pot-pourri is to be packed in clear boxes or jars for presentation, first press a few daisies between sheets of newsprint or in dry sand so that these can be displayed pressed 'open-eyed' against the glass or box cover.

Cherry pie, *Heliotrope.* There are several species but *H. peruvianum* and *H. corymbosum* are mainly cultivated. These do not require much heat but are soon killed or damaged by cold. Good container plants as well as bedders.

Clary sages, *Salvia sclarea.* A perennial used as a fixative in perfumery and consequently useful in pot-pourri. The annual *S. horminum* has several coloured varieties with ruby, magenta, violet and purple bracts. All of these give colour to pot-pourri, but *S. sclarea* is the most strongly scented.

Curry plant, *Helichrysum angustifolium.* The little button-like yellow flowers add both pungency and colour to mixtures.

Honeysuckle, *Lonicera.* To most people this means the lovely climber. However, not only the tubular flowers of these decorative kinds can be used but also the more insignificant flowers of the evergreen shrub species and varieties.

Hyssop, *Hyssopus officinalis.* This has rich blue-lipped flowers and there are varieties with pink, purple and white blooms. The foliage is also useful.

Above: 'Blue Stocking' Bergamot, or Monarda. *Below: The blue-lipped flowers of hyssop,* Hyssop officinalis. *Far right: The brilliant bloom of the honeysuckle,* Lonicera peryclymenum.

Jasmine, *Jasminum officinale.* Summer flowering. A climbing plant with very sweetly scented white flowers.

Marigold, *Calendula officinalis.* The dried petals are faintly pungent and they add an attractive note of colour to mixtures. They are especially useful for blending with leaves. Use them with a sprinkling of borage flowers for pleasant complementary colour harmony.

Marjoram, *Origanum.* Good stimulating scent when dried. Particularly useful in bath sachets with pine and lemon balm. Can also be used in pot-pourris. Leaves are also used.

Meadowsweet

Meadowsweet, *Filipendula ulmaria.* One of the strewing herbs, the smell of which, according to Gerard, 'Makes the heart merry and joyful and delighteth the senses'. Flowers and leaves are used.

Melilot, *Melilotus officinalis.* A graceful plant of the pea family, once an important fodder crop and used in brewing. The dried flowers smell of new mown hay like woodruff, for which it can be substituted if necessary.

Mock orange, *Philadelphus coronarius,* and some other fragrant species. This deserves to be used

much more widely. A good ingredient for pot-pourris but also a flower strong enough to stand on its own as a sachet filler.

Rosemary, *Rosmarinus officinalis.* If you have the patience to gather these flowers you will be well rewarded. Perfect in 'manly' spicy pot-pourris. A good shampoo herb.

(Incidentally, the suffix 'officinalis' has probably appeared here often enough to excite the curiosity of the reader. Its meaning is 'of use to man' and it will frequently be found connected with trees, shrubs and herbaceous plants, and as we see with herbs, where the plant or a part of the plant can be used, eaten, spun, woven, drunk or otherwise employed.)

Sweet Cicely, *Myrrhis odorata.* The white umbels retain their sweet soft perfume after drying.

Tansy

Tansy, *Tanacetum vulgare.* This has yellow, button-like flowers which are pleasantly pungent. The leaves also can be used, but with discretion.

Thymes, Thymus. Flowers and leaves from any species or variety of thyme can be used in pot-pourri.

Woodruff, *Asperula odorata.* A charming little ground cover

plant which will smother the soil under trees and shrubs. The dried flowering stems smell of new mown hay.

Wallflowers, *Cheiranthus cheiri.* Begin the pot-pourri making process in late spring by gathering plenty of these.

Generally speaking for flowers one should mix some seven-

Wallflowers

eighths of any flower petals to one-eighth of dried leaves, measured by bulk, to a summer pot-pourri mixture. With these, fixatives should be used.

The number of scented leaves is many. Some plants from which these can be gathered are as follows.

Ambrosia, *Chenopodium ambrosioides.* This is an annual known as Mexican tea. Both leaves and seeds can be used in leafy mixtures.

Angelica, *Angelica archangelica.* All parts of this plant are fragrant.

Artemisia. These are scented relatives of the pungent tarragon with evocative names such as lad's love or southernwood, *A. abrotanum.*

Not such pretty names are wormwood and mugwort, but their leaves are pungent and clean smelling. Like other artemisias they were once used to repel moths and fleas. Southernwood is called 'garde-robe' in French. *A. absinthium* is the common wormwood. *A. vulgaris* is mugwort. Roman wormwood or small absinth is *A. pontica*.

These are decorative plants as well as fragrant ones in a garden. Many are delightfully silvery and some have forms which are even more silver and worth searching for, especially if you hope to make a silver border. *A. tridentata*, the sage brush, grows really tall, some six to eight feet high and has a beautiful silver sheen as well as a sweet fragrance. More about these can be found in the chapter on the connoisseur's garden.

Balm, *Melissa officinalis*. The lemon-scented leaves should be dried quickly if they are to retain their scent. Gather them before the plant flowers. They need mixing with a fixative.

Basil, Basilicum. The varieties purple basil, grand violet and dark opal are best for pot-pourri.

Bay, *Laurus nobilis*. Surprisingly perhaps this is an important ingredient in pot-pourri.

Catmint

Catmint, *Nepeta cataria*. This really is for cats! Use the dried leaves to stuff cat 'toys', muslin mice, fish and balls, if you are so inclined.

Cotton lavender

Cotton lavender, *Santolina chamaecyparissus*. Dried and made into sachets this is an effective moth-repellant.

Geranium

Geranium, scented. This name is botanically correct only when applied to the hardy species of herbaceous geranium. Those which are pot grown, though widely known by this name, are in fact pelargoniums and can be found listed as such.

The leaves of most of the garden species and varieties appear to be scented to some degree, and in some cases stems and roots also. Certainly when one bruises a plant while gardening it gives off its own characteristic scent. Even the blue flowered *G. pratense* does this. Some are much more strongly scented than others. Of them all, *G. macrorrhizum* is the most popular.

Lemon verbena, *Lippia citriodora*. A deciduous shrub or small tree which is not entirely hardy. In cold areas it should be protected in winter.

Mignonette

Mignonette, *Reseda odorata*. No other flower has quite the same haunting perfume. The plant grows best under cool conditions whether in the garden or in a greenhouse or conservatory. It is a good container plant and prefers a rich, rather heavy soil. In the garden it is said to thrive best when a good amount of old mortar rubble is added to the soil, but I have seen it growing excellently without this and in any case who today can conveniently lay his hands on old mortar rubble?

Mint, Mentha species. There are some mints whose leaves are so fragrant that they are more suitable for perfumery than for cookery. However, this does not of course exclude them. One form of apple mint, the pretty *Mentha rotundifolia variegata*, is delicious in salads. It is particularly sweetly scented with a fruity aroma. *M. citrata* is the bergamot mint which produces a lemon-scented oil. Its synonym is *M. odorata*.

Much confusion exists about the names of the many varieties and I suspect that people tend to have their own names for many mints. They are known as eau-de-cologne, pineapple, citrus, orange and several others. All have really strong scents and I suggest that when in doubt you buy a plant on the strength of its scent rather than merely on that of its name.

Dried mint leaves are useful in pot-pourri and sachet mixtures. In a copy of Dickens' *Home Notes* for May, 1896, under the heading 'Sweet Fumigation', appears this information. 'It is said that the best plants to be cultivated for the purpose of disinfection are the cherry-laurel, clove and lavender, and the best herbs are mint and thyme. Narcissus, hyacinth and mint are also recommended.'

Pot geranium, Pelargonium. Many of the species have scented leaves. Usually their blooms are not highly decorative and cannot be compared with the showy zonal pelargoniums of our tubs and window-boxes. However, many are attractive plants just the same and will last for years. Generally speaking they are best treated as contained plants and this applies whether grown in a greenhouse or out of doors. They are not

Above: Mentha aquatica.
Below: Mentha spicata, *or spearmint. Just two of the many varieties of mint. If you do not know all their right names, choose them by their scent.*

Right: The vivid petals of this pelargonium, sometimes called geranium, when dried would add a splash of colour to a pot-pourri.

hardy and must be brought indoors or given adequate protection if there is danger of frost.

They are easily propagated from cuttings.

The most popular of all is the so-called 'rose' geranium, *Pelargonium graveolens*. There are two kinds, the large-leaved and the small-leaved. Foliage is grey-green, usually heart-shaped but sometimes rounder than this. The essential oil from this plant is used as an adulterant for Attar of Roses, but *P. capitatum* is known as the Attar of Roses geranium. Very widely grown is the pretty variegated, curly leaved *P. crispum* with a melissa-like lemon scent. *P. fragrans* is the nutmeg-scented geranium; *P. x nervosum* is lime-scented; *P. odoratissimum* smells of apples; *P. denticulatum* of minty roses; the downy *P. tomentosum* is pepperminty; *P. quercifolium*, known as the oak-leaved geranium on account of the shape of its leaves, is pleasantly yet undefinably scented.

Oak-leaf geranium

It has also given rise to many varieties which vary in the nature of their scents as well as in their intensity.

The leaves are used in a small way in cooking. Leaves of the rose geranium (and I have used others including the oak-leaved variety) can be pressed on the floor of a greased sponge sandwich tin and the cake batter poured over them. In the baking they will impart their flavour to the sponge. It makes a refreshing change from the ubiquitous vanilla. I like to

Crispum

use the leaves of crispum when making apple jelly. A sprig or two is thrown in during the last few minutes when the liquid is boiling fast. This also improves the flavour. The leaves can be sugar-frosted for cake decoration.

All of the dried leaves are good sachet herbs, and incidentally I have toyed from time to time with the dried leaves of the zonal varieties and found them good in a spicy mixture. The basic mixture for a sachet to lay among clothes is one part rose geranium, one lemon verbena (or alternatively *P. crispum* leaves which more people are likely to have) and one part lavender.

St John's wort, *Hypericum patulatum*, and its varieties such as *Henryi*. The fresh evergreen leaves and stems have a resinous tangerine scent which is retained when the leaves are dried.

Sun rose, *Cistus ladaniferus*. The gum cistus has aromatic leaves. This, like others of its kin, is a good rock garden shrub. It needs a sheltered place and light, well drained soil.

This, then, is a selection of plants you can grow from which you can hope to gather ingredients for perfume. It is possible that you have others in your garden or perhaps in your locality which can also be used. Dry a few as a sample and do not judge them quickly. Sometimes the fragrance is not noticeable until the flower, leaf, root or seed ages. Orris root is a good example of this. Coriander seed is another.

Orris root figures largely in many recipes, even in old mouth sweeteners and dentifrices. The *Home Notes* correspondent already referred to describes its use thus: 'A good handful of orris root soaked in spirits of wine will manufacture a delightful toilet water. Take a bottle with a wide neck and mouth, fill it halfway with lumps of orris root and saturate these in a bath of spirits of wine which reaches to the neck

of the bottle. Shake well every day, but leave the mixture for a week, or better still a fortnight, before it is used. Strain and pour it off into small bottles and cork them tightly. The orris root may yet be sufficiently fragrant to bear a second bath of spirits of wine, but in this instance use only half the quantity of spirits.'

Obviously the jar should be kept covered.

It is possible to buy orris root from a chemist, even if you have to insist that he orders it. I would also suggest that you try drying and preparing your own roots, using this iris with angelica, sweet cicely and geranium. First wash the roots. Slice them, then let them dry in a very slow, barely warm oven or some other suitable place. The roots can be ground most easily in an electric grinder. Otherwise pound them in a mortar.

Obviously, if you hope to make good pot-pourri, sachets, sweet bags or whatever, it is essential that the leaves and petals you use are properly dried. Read the section on drying herbs as well as the following notes.

Petals and leaves should not only be dry when gathered but also in their prime, for then they are most fragrant. The best time, generally speaking, is just after they have come into flower.

Pot-pourri is either 'wet' or dry, although the first term is slightly misleading, for it refers to the contents rather than the condition of the mixture. In a wet pot-pourri petals and leaves are mixed with either common or bay salt, a coarse, large-grained salt.

The basic method is as follows. Using a glass jar, the kitchen storage type with a close fitting lid, begin with a layer of petals or leaves, mixed or all of one kind, one to two inches deep. Sprinkle these with a little ground allspice and cloves, some powdered citrus peel and a little alcohol, brandy or Polish spirit. This latter acts

as a preservative. Cover this layer with salt to hide the petals completely. Add more layers in the same way until the jar is full. This

can be done daily as the ingredients become ready and are collected. Cover and keep in the dark in a cool place for at least six weeks. The pot-pourri can then be packed into suitable receptacles and placed about the house.

This makes a good, pleasant smelling and long-lasting mixture which can be refreshed from time to time either by adding a small amount of a new mixture or a few drops of one of the essential oils.

This also is a basic recipe. It can be adjusted to suit one's taste, or rather smell, and also to whatever ingredients it is possible to obtain.

An alternative method is first to dry the petals and leaves by spreading them on sheets of clean, strong paper or plastic in a clean,

airy room but not in sun or artificial heat. They should be sprinkled with the salt and turned from time to time until they are dry. They can then be layered with spices and fixatives and with only a little extra salt.

It is a good plan to prepare a quantity of spice mixture in advance. It keeps well in a closed plastic bag inside a tightly closed box. A basic recipe for a spice mixture is: two ounces of any one powdered root such as violet scented orris, angelica, khus-khus, sweet cicely or whatever you have or can get; one ounce each of cloves, powdered nutmeg (or half an ounce of the nutmeg and half an ounce of coriander) and cinnamon; half an ounce of powdered citrus peel and a few drops of any essential oil.

Sprinkle this mixture over the

layers of petals and leaves together with a sprinkling of salt, its quantity equalling the bulk of the spices.

Another spice mixture is made up of half a pound of common salt, half a pound of bay salt, half an ounce each of powdered nutmeg, cinnamon, cloves, allspice, coriander, citrus peel, gum benzoin, borax and orris root. Reserve the last until all the other ingredients have been mixed and then add it to the rest.

Although I would call these basic recipes I must say that the word would be used very loosely, for one has only to browse through some of the old books on herbs and their uses to see just how varied the recipes can be.

Consider for example, the prodigality of this one, which is included mainly out of interest, although it is perfectly practical for any reader who has a large garden. It is taken from *Domestic Cookery*, 1834.

'Put into a large China jar the following ingredients in layers, with bay salt strewed between the layers; two pecks of damask roses part in bud and part full blown; violets [obviously these would have to be gathered and dried earlier in the year, unless by violets it is violas which is meant] orange-flowers and jasmine, a handful of each; orris root sliced, benjamin [benzoin] and storax, two ounces each; a quarter of an ounce of musk; a quarter of a pound of angelica root sliced; two handfuls of lavender flowers; half a handful of rosemary flowers; bay and laurel leaves[?], half a handful each; three Seville oranges stuck as full of cloves as possible, dried in a cool oven, and pounded; half a handful of knotted marjoram; and two handfuls of balm of Gilead dried. Cover all quite close. When the pot is uncovered, the perfume is very fine.'

Here are two of the special ingredients that you would need for the exotic herb mixture we have quoted on this page. Left: The delicate white flower of jasmine, Jasminum officinale. Right: The rich colour of the attractively named Meadow Crane's bill, or Geranium pratense, will add warmth to any corner.

As you can see, recipes for pot-pourris and spice mixtures vary considerably and some seem rather involved.

One very simple mixture for pot-pourri sent to me by an American friend is as follows: four pints dried rose petal leaves, damask roses for preference; one cup mixed lemon-scented leaves, mixed or all of one kind; a quarter pound each of common salt, bay salt and brown sugar; half an ounce of gum storax, gum benzoin, orris root, cinnamon, cloves and ground citrus peel. Mix these well inside a deep jar. Stir it often, using a wooden spoon kept for this purpose. Cover until the perfume becomes strong. The jar can then be uncovered from time to time to sweeten rooms or cupboards. Alternatively, remove the pot-pourri and distribute it among pot-pourri holders.

Try my modern version of an old recipe taken from *The Toilet of Flora*. One pint of mock orange; half a pint each of modern roses, old fashioned roses and lavender flowers; a quarter pint of sweet marjoram leaves; a quarter pint of clove scented pinks or carnations; slightly less than a quarter pint of thyme; one-eighth of a pint of myrtle leaves and melilot; a tablespoon each of powdered rosemary leaves and powdered cloves; half a tablespoon of bay leaves. Mix these in a bowl and cover with strong paper as though you were covering a jar of jam. Stand in the sun for the whole summer. Stir it every other day with a wooden spoon. At the end of the season stir in an ounce or two of powdered orris root.

While pot-pourri is intended to be stood about the house, sachets are to be laid in drawers or hung in cupboards. It was believed for centuries that they deterred moths, fleas and other insects, and who shall say that this is not so. If in refusing to believe this is true we sacrifice the delicious, sweet scents of summer past, is it worth while being up to the minute and using a chemical aerosol spray instead? I think that once you have pressed lavender between your bed linen, hung a sweet bag or pomander in your wardrobe or closet, or dangled a herb bag in your bath, you will become hooked on real perfumes and will willingly forgo synthetic 20th century smells.

Make small bags of muslin to hold the sachet herbs. Incidentally, pot-pourri which has been standing in bowls for a year or two will often become 'recharged' if it is put in sachets and used in a close place.

Linen sachets

These can be as simple (i.e., filled with lavender flowers, mignonette, mock orange or rose petals) or as mixed as you wish.

I like mixed sweet scented mints, lavender and lemon verbena.

For a delightful flower scent mix equal quantities of mock orange and lavender flowers. Rose petals can be mixed with powdered cloves to give a clove carnation-like perfume. Mignonette, southernwood and woodruff is both elusive and unusual. It reminds me of those golden summer evenings when the cut hay lies in swathes in the fields.

A simple lavender sachet

Two ounces lavender flowers; one ounce ground dried rosemary leaves; two ounces orris or angelica root powder; five drops oil of rose. Mix and place in thin sachets.

Bouquet sachet

Two ounces damask rose petals; two ounces lavender flowers; two ounces mock orange or philadelphus blossoms; one ounce powdered root, orris for preference; two teaspoons each of powdered cloves, allspice, cinnamon and coriander.

Flower sachet

One pint rose petals; one pint lavender flowers; half pint marjoram; half pint eau-de-cologne or apple mint or mixed mints; half pint thyme; four ounces powdered root (orris, khus-khus, angelica or sweet cicely); two ounces caraway seed; two ounces coriander; half ounce of powdered cloves; one ounce of powdered rosemary and half an ounce of powdered bay.

Lemon sachet

(Make these into tiny sachets like bouquet garni bags and use them for scenting a bath. Store the bags in a well-stoppered jar.)

One pint lemon verbena leaves; two ounces powdered lemon peel; two ounces powdered orange peel; one ounce caraway seed; a few drops of oils of verbena, bergamot and lemon. This can be made without the oils but then is not so quickly fragrant.

Before unlimited water and wash basins and bathrooms became part of the essential home fittings, toilet waters and flower vinegars were important fresheners. They can still play that role, but after a bath now, not instead of it! All flower vinegars can be made by putting three ounces of flower petals or leaves in a jar and covering them with a quart of best wine vinegar. Rose, lavender and violet seem naturals, but try mignonette, rose geranium, jasmine and clove pink; alone, not mixed.

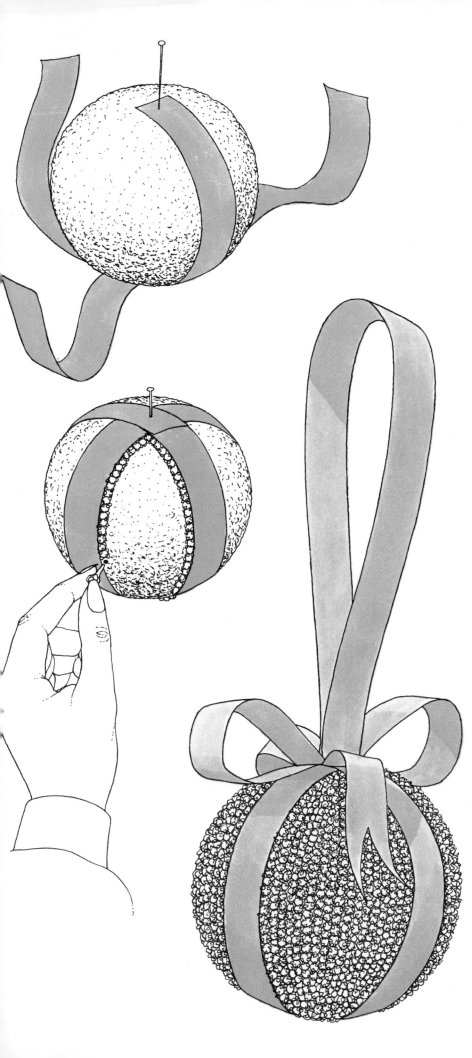

Pomander

And finally the pomander. Seville oranges are best for this but since their season is brief and in some countries they are not available at all, in their place use instead a ripe, thick-skinned orange. Take two lengths of narrow tape and wrap these around the orange so that they divide it into four sections. Pin or staple the ends in place at the flower end of the fruit. These are to be removed later and replaced with more attractive ribbon. Have ready a quantity of cloves. These are to be stuck into the orange and should cover it really closely with no spaces left between the clove heads.

First follow the tape edges around so that you get a nice, even pattern. If you find it difficult to pierce the skin of the orange with the clove, use a cuticle stick to make a hole first. When the orange is entirely covered have ready orris root powder and cinnamon mixed together. Failing these make some other spicy mixture such as ground allspice and nutmeg or coriander. Put the powder in a paper bag. Put the covered orange in the bag. Close the top, hold it firmly and shake the fruit so that the powder sticks closely to it.

Leave it in the bag, or alternatively wrap it in tissue, and stow it away in the airing cupboard or in some other dry atmosphere out of the light for two or three weeks. When you take it out remove the tape and replace it with smart ribbon, making a loop to suspend the pomander.

I like to hang pomanders in a clothes cupboard. The smell is spicy and clean, quite suitable for a man's wardrobe.

The orange should grow harder and harder, and smaller.

57

There are literally dozens of things you can do with herbs which must surely be the most versatile of all plants. Indeed, this very versatility of herbs almost certainly accounts for their popularity from the very earliest times.

Herbs were not only an invaluable – indeed, the staple – part of the apothecary's craft and an invaluable aid to good cooking, they also gave the housewife a chance to fashion many useful and delightful trivialities in the winter months that added to the gaiety of living.

Tussie-mussies, bookmarks, pomanders, corsages, sachets, toys for cats, drawer pillows, scent for the bath, rose jars, special pillows to induce a fragrant and delicious slumber with 'evil spirits' kept firmly away – the infinitely adaptable herb was a source of many delights. Herbs even provided some excellent hair rinses and, of course, these rinses combined with soft rainwater from a cottage water-butt are today among the more exotic and fragrant memories of things past. There is a certain cachet in using what amounts to a medieval shampoo!

So let us try in this chapter to offer a few suggestions. And since herbs seem peculiarly the province of the lady of the house, let's begin with the beauty aids.

Rose Vinegar

Rose vinegar makes a splendid skin astringent. The preparation is very simple. Collect one ounce of Damask rose petals and steep them in half a pint of white wine vinegar. Leave this brew for a couple of weeks in a sunny place and then strain off the liquid. Add half a pint of rose water to this. Select some attractive bottles – for everything to do with herbs

Two beautiful and very different roses. On the left: the rich blooms of Rosa mundi. *On the right: the simple, white blooms of* Philadelphus Beauclerk.

these details are important because they heighten the mystique and the delight – pour the liquid into the bottles, cork and leave to settle for a while. The result is a remarkably efficient and pleasant skin astringent.

Scented rose petals can also be used, of course, as the basis for a fragrant toilet water.

Rose Vinegar for Toilet Use

Rose vinegar for toilet use should be made in the following manner:

Take a glass jar and half fill the jar with scented rose petals. Pour white wine vinegar over these until the jar is full. Cover this mixture and let it stand in the hot sun for several days. Actually at least twenty-four hours of full sunshine exposure is necessary, so count up the sunshine hours. Once the sun has done its work strain off the liquid in your jar and bottle. You can use the result for a variety of purposes. Try a little in the washing water to add an overall and indefinably delicate perfume to the clothes. And if you have a headache soak a tissue in this chilled and soothing mixture and apply to the forehead, thereby demonstrating once again the adaptability of herbs.

Hair Rinse

Now for a hair rinse. For this particular rinse – a great favourite of ours – you need rosemary sprigs. Simmer a clutch of sprigs in a saucepan of rain water but use only sufficient water to cover the sprigs. That point is important. From then onwards use your nose! Take a gentle sniff from time to time and when the liquid is scented to your taste – or rather preference – strain the contents of the pan and bottle the liquid. You will have a particularly refreshing hair rinse that will add a suitably fragrant lustre to your hair.

If your hair is fair and you want to brighten it up a little repeat the operation described above but this time use chamomile sprigs instead.

Herb Bath

And now to the bath and that ultimate luxury of herb scented bathwater. For this a wide range of herbs can be used. Begin with a basic stockpile of dried lemon verbena rosemary, bergamot or the other mints, lavenders, rose geraniums, lemon balm, sweet marjoram. Gather in other herbs as the fancy takes you. You can, of course, try a mixture of the whole or select only those you feel will give you the particular fragrance you covet. You can collect separate bottles of different herbs and become your own perfume manufacturer. Whichever herb or mixture of herbs you select, the technique is the same. Steep, say, half a cupful in boiling water or even more if you care to wallow deeply in your bath.

Let the herbs remain in the boiling water for about a quarter of an hour and then strain off the liquid into the bathwater. The result should be bliss – if you have made the right selections, and this skill you can acquire with practice.

Bath Bags

Bath bags, incidentally, make quite delightful gifts and they are so simple to make. Sew up some bags from cheesecloth – vary the shapes to suit your tastes or to flatter your inventive capacity – and then simply fill them with your favourite dried herbs. Put the bags into attractive glass jars and you have a charmingly personalised present. However, to avoid any unfortunate misuses of your gift it might be as well to label it clearly 'for the bath'!

Herb Incense

So much for herbs strained off in liquids. You can also use herbs as an incense. In this area dried rosemary, lavender, sage or southernwood are particularly effective. Burned in an incense burner these herbs quickly add freshness to a stuffy sick-room and can also be extremely effective in suppressing kitchen smells.

This use of herbs was particularly popular in the Middle Ages since the herbs were thought to have an antiseptic or purifying effect. Curiously enough, modern science is for once in agreement with medieval belief for it has now been discovered that these particular herbs – and we refer to the ones we have quoted – do, in fact, contain an antiseptic oil in their makeup. So it seems our forefathers (or foremothers) knew a thing or two.

War on Moths

Herbs are also efficient moth preventitives. Bunches of fresh and pungent herbs can be hung in wardrobes and placed in drawers

to keep away moths and they are surely very much more pleasant than chemical sprays or mothballs which have such nasty manufactured connotations. If moths are to be killed or fobbed off let us do this in a civilised and even graceful manner!

Try wormwood, tansy, santo-lina or southernwood which are particularly effective. Indeed, in France the name for southernwood is 'garderobe', which makes the point quite clearly. And garderobe was in universal use in that country centuries before our nasty man-made products were contrived.

Any of the herbs we have mentioned can be dried and crushed and put into small bags to tuck strategically away among the clothes. You'll be surprised – and very gratified – to discover how effective they can be.

Sachets

In the same sort of general area of adding a delicate perfume to a drawer and bringing a whiff of cottage-style air and freshness to your home, you can make your favourite sweet smelling herbs into sachets and pop these into drawers or linen cupboards.

Now the sachet should not only deliver a lingering and delicate perfume, it should also be a contrivance of great beauty and delicacy in itself. There is a whole aesthetic on the making of sachets and infinite scope for skill and general artistry. Lavender or pot-pourri or any sweetly-smelling herbs are, as we have said, the ingredients to be used, but selecting the contents is only half the fun. Your true sachet-maker honours the herbs she has chosen by lavishing skill and affection on their containers.

Any thin and preferably see-through material will do for the bag itself and you may fashion the bag into any shape that pleases you. No matter that it is to be hidden away among the clothes. Don't forget that it will be received as a gift and your sachets must be rare delights.

Fashion them, for example, into heart shapes. Embroider them if you really want to display your skills – maybe with a flower motif to symbolise the herbs within –

and then trim them with delicate lace. A twist of ribbon can also be added to give additional charm. The result is a sachet fit to slip into the drawer of any lady in the land.

A Sleep Pillow

And now, as Pepys (himself an admirer of herbs) would say, to bed – and what better or more original gift than a sleep pillow?

Hop pillows were used for many centuries in England as sleep inducers. They were a great favourite with King George III who, poor man, needed all the sleep he could get. But they are also helpful to asthma sufferers – and that isn't just an old wive's tale. Dried hops alone are used to fill standard-sized pillows and these are then used instead of ordinary feather-packed pillows.

The Americans did things rather differently but with the same aim in mind. They used balsam pine to stuff their sleep pillows and usually advocated small pillows or sachets about six inches by four in area – just big enough to place gently under one's cheek.

Tussie-Mussies

Now no account of these infinitely possible uses of herbs would be complete without mentioning the tussie-mussie, surely the most traditional and attractive of all herb decorations, adornments and devices. Our illustrations show you some examples of these herb bouquets.

Tussie-mussies are part of the tradition of Olde Englande. They have been carried at Coronations and, indeed, no less a lady than Elizabeth II was actually handed a tussie-mussie as she entered Westminster Abbey for her Coronation.

In the long, long ago when plagues and fevers troubled the land, tussie-mussies were held to ward off noxious smells and illness-bearing aromas of all kinds.

Favourite herbs selected for tussie-mussies varied from period to period. The 15th Century, for example, was partial to marigold since the brightly shining marigold, which 'dedicated its beauty to the sun', was a symbol for happiness and sunshine. Then again they believed in sentiment in those days and heartsease, which symbolised the remembrance of things past, was another firm favourite. In the same genre were forget-me-nots and southernwood wrapped round a deep red rose bud. Who could deny love, devotion and the tenderer feelings when handed such a tussie-mussie?

Often sprays of southernwood were tucked into a ladies' corsage before going to church. Then, again, the white and gold flowers of camomile flanking a sprig of sage were evidence of wisdom and the serenity of long years.

Part of the fun of making tussie-mussies and using them as gifts is writing the significance or meaning of the herbs used on your gift card. Lavender for luck, lily-of-the-valley for purity. Your medieval lass knew to a fine shade the precise message of the gift.

Make your bouquet or tussie-mussie by choosing the small, delicate flowers. The tussie-mussie has something of the refined artistry of a miniature painting and every leaf, flower and sprig, counts. Small roses, clove pinks, forget-me-nots, violets are perfect for your purposes. Above all, avoid making your tussie-mussie too large or cumbersome.

Choose, we suggest, a rose-bud for your central flower. Or, failing this, three or five lavender stems tied together.

Next arrange a circle of flowers,

Right: Old China Blush Ros

These attractive tussie-mussies include, left, a rosebud, sage, rue, thyme and lemon balm, and right, a collection of scented leaves and sentimental flowers.

or flowers alternating with leaves, round the centre.

As you do this, bind the stems. Repeat the process with another circle of contrasting flowers if possible. Bind these also as you proceed to build-up your tussie-mussie. Put, perhaps, a ring of eau de Cologne mint, southern-wood or some scented leaves outside this circle. Bind the stems neatly. Then trim. Have a little paper doily or a circle of stiff net ready and then slip the posy stem through the centre of this. And, hey presto, you will have fashioned an object of infinite delight and subtle meaning. Tie the doily or stiff net with a matching ribbon and perfection is complete.

Fragrant corsages are another contrivance, to pin into the front of your dress. Make fine-petalled flowers – you can choose your own

petal shape – out of organdie, nylon or any other thin yet pretty and non-porous cloth. Make each petal up double, like an envelope and fill with dried rose petals and dried herbs. Sew the petals together so that they form a flower and then add a few artificial leaves. If you want to add a particular flourish or to give a particular intimacy and charm to a dinner party you can tie a place card to your flowers and use them to show your guests where to sit.

Sweet Bags

Sweet bags are another old favourite although like many good things from the past they are rarely seen nowadays. Why not revive them in your home?

Sweet bags are perfumed bags similar in shape to lavender bags but usually at least six inches square. They are made up from thin material, either patterned or plain to suit your taste or decor. The important point here is that the material should obviously be thin enough and 'porous' enough to allow the scent of the herbs to seep through.

In the old days these sweet bags were hung on the backs of chairs or on the heads of beds to give fragrance to the room. And very effective they were!

The ingredients for your sleep bags can include any dried sweet-smelling flowers, herbs, spices and fixatives. In essence there is really no difference between the filling for a sweet bag and the herbs used for a dry pot-pourri.

The American Museum at Claverton in England, which is versed in all the lore and craft of herbs, uses more herbs and less spices than in the Museum's standard pot-pourri. They always include lavender, rosemary and rose leaves, lemon verbena or lemon balm, mint and marjoram.

Spices such as cinnamon and cloves may also be added but

always in small quantities.

It is best to go on mixing and adding until you have the particular perfume that you find pleasing. We suggest you add an ounce of fixative (that is to say, gum benzoin or orris) to about one pound of the dried mixture.

Made into flat pillows or sachets, your sweet bags can be tucked into all sorts of places, such as under cushions or even down the sides of sofas and chairs.

Cat Toys

Perhaps we should mention herbs as cat toys! Yes, that infinite variety of uses again. Get the artist in your family to draw a simple outline of a mouse – not

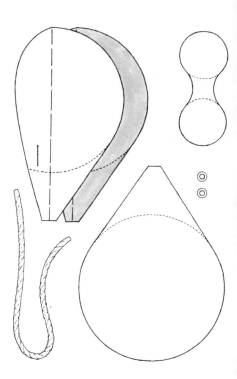

Using one 12″ square of cotton, cut out pieces to measurements shown, leaving two small slits in top pieces (B) for ears. Sew the two top pieces together around top edge. Place top and base (A) right side together and stitch, leaving small gap at rounded edge for filling. Turn to right side. Roll ears into pencil. Shape and thread through slits in top. Fill with catnip. Insert string in gap and sew up. Sew on beads as eyes. Use cotton for whiskers.

too complicated – on a piece of suitable material. Sew the outlines together, leave a small opening and fill your mouse with dried catnip. Then, of course, sew up the

opening. You can also make him a cushion of catnip but he'll have hours of fun patting away at the mouse.

Herb Teas

From cat toys to herb tea is a large jump but then herbs are full of surprises. Herb teas are justifiably famous and they have a long and ancient lineage. The technique is as follows:

Steep the dried leaves or flowers in boiling water for at least five minutes. Jasmine flowers, lime flowers, chamomile flowers, leaves of sage, mint or bergamot all make splendid teas. Indeed, aromatic flowers or leaves can also be used.

If steeping fails to bring out the flavour, the herbs can be boiled for a few minutes.

A number of herb teas can be taken medicinally such as sage, or lemon for colds, peppermint or lovage for nervous exhaustion and fennel or caraway for indigestion.

Candied Violets

Finally, a great delicacy – candied violets. And for these you should use only perfect flowers. Here's the technique:

Wash the flowers lightly and dry them off on a piece of kitchen paper. Leave them, in other words, on the paper and let them dry by themselves.

Then heat up the white of an egg. Then take a fine brush and

paint each flower with the egg white so that it is perfectly covered. Then carefully dust each one with caster sugar until it is well coated. Dust some greaseproof paper with a little sugar and then lay your flowers on this to dry. Here we should give you a tip. It is best to lay the paper on baking sheets or on a sieve, so that the flowers will not move when they are shifted from place to place during their preparation.

Once the flowers are coated, snip off their stems. It's a good idea to leave the stems on up to this point since they will prove easier to handle than if you snip them off at any earlier stage.

Place the trays in an airing cupboard or in some other warm, *dry* place. But *NOT* – repeat, *NOT* – in the sun, for twenty-four hours or even a little longer than this if the flowers are not quite dry.

Then you are ready. Store the candied violets away in jars, placing a little greaseproof paper between each layer, and the ultimate gourmet's confection will be ready for your favourite guests.

Lavender Hat

But if you want a final herb contrivance to cap the lot, if we may coin a pun, you could always try a lavender hat and put it up for sale at some local bazaar!

For this you must cut a circle out of some attractive, stiff material to serve as a base for the lavender bag and also as a brim for the 'hat'.

Then cut a small circle of muslin. Mark a slightly smaller circle

in the centre of the crown. Fill this area with lavender flowers and cover these with the muslin. Pin this in place so that the muslin covers the flowers and so that, at the same time, it looks like the crown of a hat.

Chain-stitch round the marked circle. Then add a little bow or some other touch of decoration – maybe a sprig of lavender – and you have a most ingenious gift for your bazaar.

The Families of Herbs

Throughout the centuries and by common consent some herbs and spices have been more favoured for certain foods than others. Why this should have been so is interesting to speculate. Taste must have entered into this and one would have expected there to be more discrimination as the number of cultivated herbs and spice imports grew. But there are a few all-rounders such as parsley, thyme and bay, and in former years more than now, sage, which were used with any kind of meat or fish. One cannot help wondering, if these, why not others? Why do we have mint with lamb, fennel with fish, horse-radish with beef–and horse!

No doubt the medicinal qualities and the virtues of the plant were once taken primarily into account. It would have been discovered or imagined that one herb was more likely quickly and effectively to prevent a stomach disorder, or indeed actual disease and maybe worms, when served with one kind of meat than would another herb, and so it became customary to use it. Meats that were only cooked when there was an R in the month called for hardy herbs if these were to be eaten fresh, and so sage

Left: Thyme in flower. Thyme has always been one of the most reliable all-rounders, used for both fish and meat dishes. Thyme tea is another favourite.

Above: Fennel flowers, Foeniculum vulgare. Fennel is traditionally used with fish but try it with certain meats as well. Used carefully it adds a pleasant flavour.

67

and pork inevitably go together.

Magic would also have entered into it, and perhaps the origins of what plants to use lie far back in history, maybe even as far back as tribal totem animals. We are not likely ever to know if this is so. Observation must also have played a major role. The herbs chosen must often have been not only those plants which were near at hand but also those on which the animal was seen to browse with enjoyment, and the reverse would have been true. Take as an example of this an extract from Erasmus' *Convivium Religiosum*, where he makes the guests saunter before their meal around a well kept garden. "The place is dedicated to the honourable pleasures of rejoicing the eye, refreshing the nose and renewing the spirit. Only sweet scented herbs grow therein; the plants are set out in the most perfect order; every species has its own place and each one has its own *vexillum* with its name and special virtues. Thus for example speaks the marjoram, 'Keep away from me, swine: my scent is not for you', for although this plant has a sweet smell, swine cannot endure its scent." If this is really true, it might be one explanation why sage and not marjoram is the pork herb.

Nowadays there is such a great exchange of ideas and recipes that it is only to be expected that there is also more experiment. Recently I read of a special steak with tarragon, for which a certain Swiss restaurant is famous. This is not a usual combination, but it must be good since it has been recorded. It might have come about by accident. Many of us have had happy culinary accidents. Certainly if I did not have the herb a certain recipe called for I would try something else rather than use no herb at all. Sometimes the result is so good that one repeats the recipe and so a new dish is created.

However, and especially for

Hyssop

those who are just beginning to enjoy the pleasures of preparing food, it must be said that experiment is not essential. Herbs are roughly grouped into those which are most suitable for fish or for certain meats. Those who like to play safe can be assured that these are the 'correct' herbs. As a gardener as well as a cook I have been bound to notice that they fall nicely into plant families and this is the reason for the method of classification in this chapter. I believe it will be genuinely helpful to understand and appreciate these classifications, strangely botanical and technical though they may seem to be at first.

UMBELLIFERAE

The herbs most used for fish belong to the Umbelliferae, which contains those plants whose flowers mainly take the form of an umbrella (botanically an umbel) of blossom, such as parsley, chervil, dill, fennel and sweet cicely. And it is interesting to note that all the vegetables in this family, such as carrots, parsnips and sweet or Florence fennel are naturals with fish also. Their seeds or spices are good, too: dill, cumin, caraway, celery, sweet cicely, fennel are all extremely wholesome. Botanically they are usually 'fruits' although we commonly call them 'seeds'.

However, if your knowledge of plants is limited, remember please that although so many of them are so good and succulent, it does not follow that all members of this family are good to eat. Some of them like the hemlock are very poisonous indeed, even though you may find it listed in some old herbals. Nor does it follow that all parts of the culinary kinds are edible. In many cases – and celery is a good example – one can eat every part of the plant, but this is not the general rule. Incidentally, the reason why dark green celery leaves are discarded by some people is simply because unless these are blanched while they

Salad Burnet

are growing they can be very indigestible. However, they need not be wasted. They can be used in stockpots, stews and soups. Parsnip leaves, for instance, are highly indigestible, yet you can eat both the leaves and the roots of parsley. Carrot leaves are bitter yet their roots are sweet. So in the main this is a family whose members you should get to know really well before you take any chances and begin experimenting with wild plants or parts of plants for which you can find no recipe in any cook book.

Parsley

Rather than go through the list alphabetically I will begin with the best known umbellifer, parsley, *Petroselinum crispum*.

Because this has been so widely used as a garnish (and I fear usually thrown away after decorating a plate of sandwiches) we expect this herb to be bright green and 'moss' curled. Yet the French parsley is nothing like so curly, although I think that its flavour is superior. Perhaps this is because the French grow the herb to eat more than to look at.

Madame Prunier, the famous fish restaurateur, says parsley is the perfect garnish. She also recommends it fried crisp and served with sole.

Wash parsley and dry it well in a cloth and it will be easier to garnish after it is chopped. Hamburgh parsley has finely flavoured roots. Greeks and Cypriots buy a great proportion of market supplies in centres such as New York, London and Paris.

As a condiment parsley is often chopped with garlic and added to the dish at the end of cooking, as in Provencale dishes. Used alone it is known as a persillade. It can be used to make sweet country wines, both still and sparkling.

Parsley is a hardy biennial, usually flowering the year after it is sown, although in certain seasons some plants may run to seed the same year. You can hamper these efforts by keeping the flowering stems picked.

Like many of the umbellifers

Parsley

the seed quickly loses its viability and should not be kept longer than possible. Where this herb is grown in a mixed border I recommend that a few plants should be allowed to grow and seed naturally. This way there is always a supply of young seedlings coming along. These can be potted and handed on to friends or grown indoors or even used in hanging baskets. Or perhaps simplest of all they can merely be transplanted in some more convenient spot.

Parsley is notoriously slow to germinate, seedlings can take up to eight weeks to appear. If some seed of a small radish, French Breakfast for instance, is sowed with them this will germinate

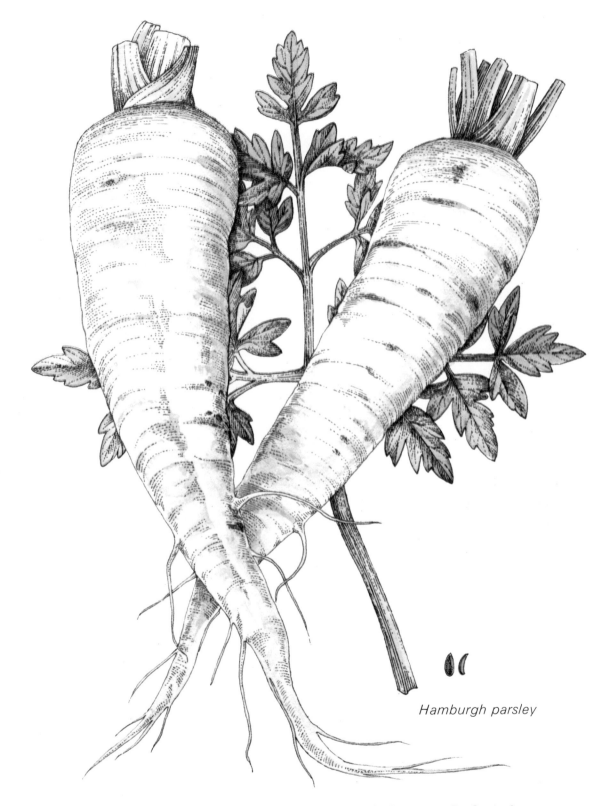

Hamburgh parsley

first and mark the spot or row where the parsley lies. The radish will be ready to pull and eat by the time the parsley seedlings appear.

If the soil is warm the seed will germinate more quickly. To this end the area can be covered with a cloche and warmed up for a few days before sowing in spring or if the weather has been particularly wet. One other method often recommended is to draw the drill and then walk along it pouring water from a kettle which has just boiled, then to sow while the drill is still warm. Probably one of the reasons for slow germination is simply that the seed is sown too deep. It should only just be covered.

Seed can be sown at any time during late spring and summer. Where much is used three sowings throughout the season are usually necessary.

To maintain a good crop soil needs to be really good and rich, well manured and yet not acid. A dressing of powdered lime or chalk will often make all the difference to a sluggish or failing crop.

Parsley can be grown under cloches in winter. Simply place these over the plants. Alternatively, lift some plants, taking care not to break the strong tap root and move them to frames or plant them in good sized pots to grow indoors.

Although more strictly a vegetable than a herb, one must list Hamburgh or Turnip-rooted parsley. It is grown mainly for its succulent and delicious roots, which are eaten much like parsnips (fine with fish!) but it is possible also to use the leaves. This is a good vegetable to grow where there is little space for either vegetables or herbs.

Chervil

Similar to parsley in appearance but more delicate in flavour – and in a way more distinctive – is chervil, *Anthriscus cerefolium*.

This is one of the ingredients in *fines herbes* and is delicious too when chopped and used either alone or with other herbs in sauces and salads. As I suggested earlier, sometimes it pays to use a 'fish herb' elsewhere. Try chopped chervil in seasoned cream with cold chicken. Like many other herbs chervil must be introduced into a dish only at the last moment or else served as a condiment, because it quickly loses its colour when cooked and is then unattractive although the taste remains.

It is a hardy annual, 12 to 18 ins. tall, often becoming biennial. The flowers are extremely dainty, like Queen Anne's lace, and charming for cutting and pressing. Chervil likes medium light soil and some shade, although I find that the self-sown plants seem to have no particular preference, many of them growing profusely where they should not, on a dry stony path or around tree boles.

The self-sown plants seem to be best in very early spring and can be gathered from late winter onwards. These flower in spring. For a constant supply it is best to sow the seed in small quantities in succession from early spring to autumn. A good rule is to sow some more when the preceding sowing appears above the soil. Cut the plants to the ground when you gather the leaves; more will soon be produced. They should be ready to cut six to eight weeks after sowing. Seed can be sown in frames or under cloches or in boxes in a greenhouse for winter supplies from autumn onwards. In hot weather or in dry conditions sow the seed in a cool, semi-shady place and water them well and frequently.

Chervil will not thrive if transplanted.

Sweet cicely

With a flavour very similar, sweet cicely, *Myrrhis odorata*, is a hardy perennial some two to three feet tall and flowering with lacy white umbels in spring.

The anise flavour of this herb is more pronounced than that of chervil and because of this it is sometimes known as anise chervil, Spanish chervil, giant sweet chervil and myrrh. Both roots and leaves of sweet cicely can be eaten, the former should be boiled. They are delicious cold, sliced and mixed with a vinaigrette dressing. The leaves can be used in the same way as chervil. The seeds are used as a spice and like caraway seed they go well with cabbage, especially red cabbage.

Sweet cicely appears to have been a real household herb at one time. Its seed was once used in wax to scent oak furniture and floors.

This herb grows easily from seed. Plants also can be divided.

Fennel

The fennels provide herbs and vegetables and salads, the latter being provided by the swollen-stemmed variety, *Foeniculum vulgare* var. *dulce*, known as Florence fennel and finnochio. This is sometimes cooked in stock and I have had it served with veal – and enjoyed it. The bulbs are usually eaten the same way as celery and the thinly sliced portions are often

Chervil

Sweet Cicely

Fennel

Dill

to be found in mixed salads in Italy. Incidentally, these 'bulbs' keep well if they are wrapped in plastic and laid on a cool floor or in some other cool place. Their leaves can be used in just the same way as the taller *F. vulgare.* There is also another variety of the type, also Italian, *F. vulgare* var. *piperitum,* whose young stems are eaten raw.

Young stems of the ordinary fennel may also be eaten. They can also be cooked like asparagus. These should be gathered and peeled just before the flowers open. For salads let them cool and serve with a dressing in which some of their leaves have been blended. Once you have used

fennel I think that you would not wish to be without it. I like to use a sprig with lemon thyme and marjoram when poaching fish. Chopped fennel leaves make a good garnish for canned fish such as sardines. The taste seems to blend especially well with lemon and I like to use the two together in sauces. Switch the herbs occasionally and use fennel with hard-boiled eggs.

Fennels are very handsome garden plants and easy to grow. The green leaves are like great soft plumes. I grow the bronze-leaved variety with them and find the contrast of hues very pleasing. The coloured variety can be eaten.

Both grow between four and six feet tall. Plants can be raised from seed and there are usually well grown plants on sale at good garden centres. They thrive in almost any kind of soil. If the flower stems are kept cut the plant will continue to produce new leaves, but of course you must let some bloom if you want to save seeds. When the plants die down gather and dry some of the stems. Fish can be laid on these and grilled (broiled) to give a very special flavour.

Dill

Dill, *Peucedanum graveolens,* is often overlooked as a fish herb yet

Angelica

it blends and savours as well as the others. It has a faintly sweet taste. It is good in canned fish pâtés and with fresh water fish, particularly with thyme for pike. Its greatest role perhaps lies in association with the salad most used with fish, particularly with salmon – the cucumber. Indeed, it is so allied with this vegetable in dill pickles that this might be the reason it is so often overlooked for other dishes. Try chopped dill scattered over cucumber when you serve this with fish either hot or cold. Try it mixed with yoghurt in stuffed cucumber rings. Simply scoop out sections of cucumber, dice the flesh, mix with yoghurt

and dill and return to the cucumber cases. Dill seed can be used in fish sauces and with new potatoes and baby carrots served with fish or alone.

If the leaves are to be used, cut them young. They can be used to flavour peas and potatoes. Throw in a leaf or two as the vegetables are boiling.

Dill vinegar is made by steeping the seed heads in good vinegar. See the recipe section for herb vinegar instructions.

Dill is an annual growing 18 to 30 ins. tall and much resembling fennel. Both plants have yellow umbels but dill does not have the same magnificence as the peren-

nial. It should be sown where it is to flower in late spring and the plants should later be thinned to about six inches apart. They are sometimes spindly plants and in some districts where the prevailing wind is strong it might be wise to support them with twiggy sticks when they are small so that they can grow up through them and be protected. The plants grow best in the sun.

Harvest the seeds as you would for caraway.

Angelica

Angelica, *Angelica archangelica*, may not be the most important herb from the culinary point of

75

view but it is certainly a handsome plant. And what a splendid name! It was given, so it is said, for the plant's angelic healing qualities, although how it was applied appears to have become lost in the mists of time. It does best and grows fastest and most lush in rich, moist loam and in light shade, and does well on an alkaline soil. It is a biennial which if prevented from flowering becomes a perennial, and flowers in late spring, growing from three to six feet tall. The whole plant is fragrant. Once it has flowered it begins to die. Obviously the thing to do is to have a stock of young seedlings ready. These are best when self-sown, and should be transplanted when still quite small, for larger plants do not always transplant satisfactorily. The stored seed quickly loses its viability, so sow it soon after it ripens, in early autumn if possible, or the following spring.

This herb has a sweeter taste than most and is used in confectionery. Possibly angelica is best known as a sweetmeat. One often sees the pieces of green candied stem decorating cakes, desserts and other goodies. Large stems are used, taken usually from plants about three years old and consequently thick. The entire stem is cut down and divided into sections. These are boiled, peeled and candied by being boiled again in a syrup of sugar and water.

The thick-peeled leaf stems are also cooked with rhubarb and they counteract the acidity of this stem while imparting their own delicate flavour. These stems are also good to nibble raw or to mix in salads. The midribs of the large leaves stripped of the foliage can be eaten like celery. Roots are also edible and these are served as a vegetable in some countries. The fruits – the seeds – are used both for flavouring food and in perfumery. They can be used in potpourris as can the dried angelica root.

Anise

Caraway

Anise

Anise, *Pimpinella anisum*, which is an annual, is another confectionery herb, used mainly for making liqueurs. Often the entire plant is used. The seeds are also used in seed cakes in the same way as caraway. Aniseed balls are boiled sugar candies flavoured with anise and with a seed at the very centre. The herb's powers of allaying digestive disorders have long been appreciated. Cakes made with aniseed and cumin were offered at the end of a meal in Roman times, no doubt a highly necessary precaution.

The leaves are edible and can be used in salads or as a pot herb. It is said that made into a pack they will remove freckles. Seeds are also sometimes used to flavour soups.

The seed can be sown outdoors in spring where the plants are to grow. They should be harvested in late summer and treated in the same way as caraway.

Caraway

Caraway, *Carum carvi*, is a biennial, and so you must sow the seed one spring to see the plant in flower the next. The seeds, really half fruits, do not all ripen at the same time but in succession, usually in early summer. Cut the stems as they become ripe. Tie them in small bunches and hang them in a clean, dry, warm and airy place above clean spread paper or paper lined trays on which the seed can drop and be collected.

Caraway taste is unpleasant to some and much enjoyed by others. While I quite like it in some fish dishes and with cabbage sometimes, I have a Hungarian friend who likes beef flavoured with caraway seeds. They are used mainly in confectionery and cakes. Caraway dislikes cold and wet conditions.

Coriander

Coriander, *Coriandrum sativum*, is one of the prettiest umbellifers,

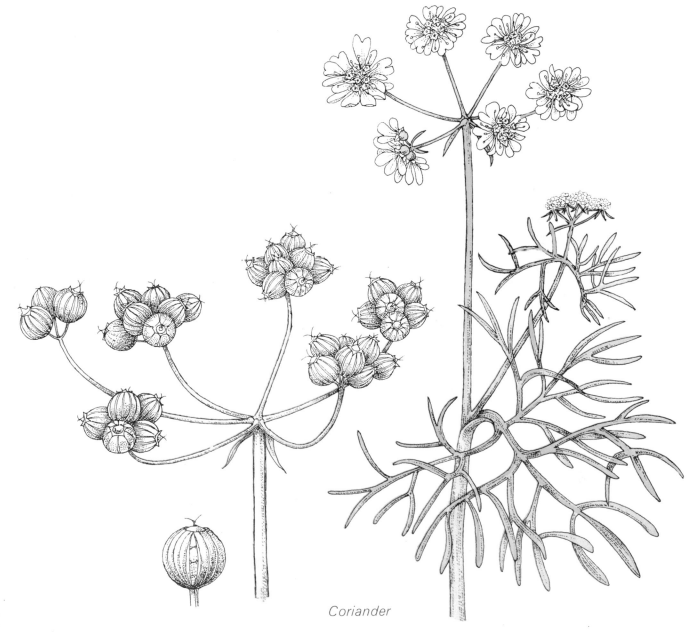

Coriander

Sage

its flowers a soft lavender mauve. It is an annual, 18 to 24 inches tall. It flowers in late summer. As soon as the first seeds are ripe the plants should be cut like caraway. Do not be repelled by the slightly unpleasant scent emanating from the drying stems. The seeds remain sweet and aromatic.

They are highly prized for flavouring liquor, especially gin. When I was a girl, coriander candies were sold. These were oddly shaped crumbs of coloured sugar with a coriander seed in the centre. I remember that it was sweet and pleasantly crunchy. Coriander is an ingredient of mixed spice. In some countries it is baked in bread. It is an important part of a curry. Coriander can be used to add distinctive flavourings to junkets and milk puddings.

Cumin

Cumin, *Cuminum cyminum*, is a very dainty little half-hardy annual with small rose coloured or white umbels. The seed mainly is used and I have not been able to find any reference to the use of leaves or root. It is an important ingredient in some curries. I prefer it to caraway, fennel or dill and I use it sometimes in fish pâtés, in some sauces and always in fish soufflés. A good pinch of seed is usually sufficient.

The seeds should be sown in late spring where the plants are to flower. You should gather the fruits when they are ripe and then treat them as caraway seeds.

Lovage

Lovage, *Ligusticum scoticum*, is a hardy perennial with a strong celery flavour. The leaves can impart this flavour to soups and to court bouillon. This is an especially useful herb to have when celery is out of season. Where recipes call for a stem of celery, use instead one good lovage leaf. The leaves can also be used as a tasty additive to pot stews and similar concoctions.

The plant grows roughly two feet tall and flowers with white umbels in late summer. It seems to grow fairly well anywhere, including a tub, but it prefers a rich, moist soil. This is a really useful all-purpose herb to grow.

LABIATAE

The greatest variety of herbs that we use come from one family, the labiatae, the family of 'lipped' flowers.

Sage

Sage, *Salvia officinalis*, is an evergreen shrub 6 to 36 ins. tall and is usually perfectly hardy. It will grow in almost any garden soil except one that is very acid. It can be grown from seed sown in spring and I have had considerable success with seedlings, but more often sage is propagated from cuttings taken in early summer from three inch lengths of the growing tips or from heeled shoots pulled from the base of old plants at any time of the year, although they root quickest in the spring. They are best struck in sandy soil under a cloche in the shade. A hormone rooting powder aids quick root formation.

The common sage is very varied. The narrow-leaved form with white flowers is said by some to be the most aromatic but there are others who swear by the broad-leaved non-flowering variety. They say that because the plant does not flower all its strength goes into the foliage. Narrow-leaved forms with blue and purple flowers also exist and are good for cooking. There are also golden, variegated and purple-leaved varieties, all of which are aromatic. These are discussed elsewhere. I grow several varieties in my herb border and constantly look for others.

Many people who know next to nothing about herbs are familiar with sage. Indeed, to many I have met the *only* stuffing or forcemeat is sage and onions blended with breadcrumbs. Unfortunately this is used without discretion with every joint from lamb to chicken, often to the detriment of the meat. It certainly is the most popular of all herbs. Literally tons of sage

Lovage

Cumin

Thyme

are sold each year, most of it for stuffing.

Actually sage is much too good to be reserved for this purpose alone. It is good boiled with beans. Try it finely chopped and blended with both cottage and cream cheeses and occasionally in a salad dressing. Derbyshire sage cheese has a wide band of fresh green sage running through it and it is very good.

I prefer to sprinkle chopped fresh sage on roasts rather than stuffing them, much better incidentally if you are counting calories. Use it also on grilled (broiled) pork chops. Blend the chopped herb with a little mustard and smear this over the meat. The

mustard tenderizes the meat as well as giving it flavour.

Thyme

The common thyme is *Thymus vulgaris*. There are numerous species, most of which can be used in cooking. In this book they are classified according to their importance and you will find more details in the chapters on Herbs in the Modern Garden, Plants for Pot-pourri and Plants for the Connoisseur.

Most widely grown for culinary purposes are common thyme and lemon-scented thyme, *T. x citrio-dorus*.

Common thyme is one of our most important herbs, a real all-

rounder, used in stuffings for meats and fish, in stews, casseroles, poultry, forcemeats, marinades and soups. It is particularly good on certain vegetables, onions, the marrow family, aubergines (eggplant) and salsify.

I like to use lemon thyme for certain dishes and to provide a change in flavours. It is good with veal, poultry and baked fish. It imparts a fresh flavour to coarse fish and should always be used in a stuffing for pike. Mix it with fennel for boiled or poached fish and for a court bouillon. It can be used in any dish in which a slight lemon flavour is acceptable. It is good in sweets such as custards, creams and sorbets. It can be

Spearmint

stewed with rhubarb. You can use the young leaves in moderation in salads. It may be compounded with butters and parsley for grills (broiling). Try it on Sole Colbert. It is also used to make country wines.

Both of these thymes like a light, rather dry soil and a warm, sunny position. The plants are best renewed after about four years. They are easily raised from seed either sown in a warm border or indoors on a window-sill and planted out later. Sow in spring. The plants may also be divided in spring. Lemon thyme is a little looser in growth than the common thyme and can be layered, an easier and more foolproof means

of propagation than division. Spread the branches out from the centre and cover their stems with soil leaving just the leafy tips exposed. The stems will root into the soil. Rooted portions can then be detached and planted. Most thymes can be propagated this way and in fact will frequently propagate themselves without your assistance.

The common thyme varies a little. You might perhaps buy or be given a plant which looks unlike the one you have already, although it may smell the same. There are forms known as English Broad-leaved and French Thyme. Neither of these appear to come true from seed.

T. serpyllum is the native British thyme of which there are many varieties in cultivation and these are discussed elsewhere. When abroad or in a strange country I always try to bring home a little wild thyme to use. I enjoy its 'wild' flavour, so frequently more concentrated and zestful. All of these varieties are safe and often good to eat.

Mint
There is more to mint than one would expect. There are, for example, 40 species in the genus Mentha and some of these species have varieties. All these varieties are numbered among the perennials.

The common spearmint (the name refers to the shape of the leaf) *Mentha spicata*, the common green mint, lamb mint or green pea mint, is most widely grown and sold. Yet it is nothing like so good in flavour as the woolly-leaved, handsome *M. rotundifolia*, the apple mint. One never sees this on sale. I suspect that this has come about because like so many other downy-leaved plant materials this mint tends to wilt quickly. It grows from two to three feet, taller than the *spicata* which is from one to two feet.

There is a hybrid mint, *M.x alopecuroides*, a cross between *M. longifolia*, European mint and *M. rotundifolia* which grows also in N. and W. Asia and N. Africa. This is a good culinary mint.

Peppermint, *M. piperata*, an English native one to three feet tall, has varieties *M. officinalis*, the slender white mint, and *M. vulgaris*, with long purplish stem. This mint, which has the true flavour of bull's eyes and humbugs, for which it was once widely used, was once also widely grown. It is distilled to make peppermint cordial. A Swiss friend used to make a tisane from the leaves to cure a cold. It makes an unusually good sorbet.

The fourth mint grown for home use for centuries but not so popular today is *M. pulegium* or pennyroyal, a creeping plant some two inches high, perfect for carpeting garden areas. (See Chapter two.) In cooking it was a 'strong' herb, used chiefly in stuffings for pig puddings and in all pig offal products such as blood or black puddings and faggots, no doubt to counteract their richness since this herb was and is valued (the ancient Greeks grew and used it) as a herb to aid digestion. It was also said to discourage fleas and for that reason was used as a strewing herb.

Even this list does not exhaust the variety of useful mints. Others are described elsewhere.

Hybrid mint

Pennyroyal mint

Mint may be used in both sweet and savoury dishes. Children like sandwiches made from chopped mint and sugar slightly moistened with a little lemon or orange juice. Chopped mint can be mixed with dried fruits, currants, sultanas, candied peel and with brown sugar used to fill pastry puffs or turnovers. I make mint jelly using an apple, plum or sometimes a rhubarb jelly base. A good handful of mint is boiled with the jelly in the final stages and removed when the liquid solidifies.

During my researches on the subject of herbs I have found that recipes for mint far outnumber those for any other herb.

Once mint grows it grows apace. Often it must be kept confined. Methods of doing this are to sink a bottomless bucket into the soil to confine the mint roots within the walls of the bucket, to use metal lawn edging, tiles, bricks or plastic for the same purpose, or to grow the plant inside a large container in the soil. My own mint runs rampant, for since the herb garden is on a mound or bank I need the mint roots to hold and secure the soil. This it does perfectly. When it encroaches I simply pull it up quite ruthlessly. Mint can be lifted, divided and planted at almost any time, but this is best done in early spring. To ensure

fresh supplies during winter, lift the roots at intervals from the autumn onwards and plant them in shallow pots or boxes. Bring them indoors into a greenhouse or some other place, even a garage or warm shed. Good light intensity is not of major importance. Aim for an average temperature of about 16°C., 60°F. Water them freely as soon as growth is seen to begin. Short sprigs are usually ready in about three weeks.

I find that if you keep cutting mint and keep it from flowering you can go on cutting fresh young sprigs until the frosts. A cloche placed over nice green plants in autumn will also ensure a supply

Water mint

Basil

of fresh shoots for some weeks to come.

Basil

If you really want to know about basil, have a word with a good Italian cook! Some of the most famous Italian dishes rely for their memorable flavour on this herb. It is used in *trinette al pesto*, crushed with peccorino cheese and olive oil, in stuffed tomatoes with rice, with pizza Napolitana and in their salads.

Basil, slightly clove-flavoured, is the perfect companion to all dishes which include tomato. It once was in great demand for a certain dish, happily not now served so often, turtle soup, in which it is the essential herb. Serve basil as a garnish with beans fresh or dried, squash, zucchini and other members of the marrow family. Give a new flavour to some old roasts by bruising the leaves and using them in a stuffing for pork or for veal. Oil of basil is used in perfumery and in medicine.

There are two kinds of basil: sweet basil, *Ocimum basilicum*, 12 ins., and bush basil, *O. minimum*, six ins., which is probably a dwarf variety of the first. Both are half-hardy annuals. They will grow well in ordinary soil so long as it is rich, sunny and well drained. It is possible to lift the plants from the ground before the onset of frosts and to grow them on as pot plants in a greenhouse or on a sunny window-sill.

If you want to give more variety to your herb garden there is a dark-leaved variety of basil which is quite handsome.

Marjoram

There are several origanums or marjorams in Italian cooking. They go with all pasta and the accompanying tomato and garlic sauces, with fish, *zuppa di pesce*, shell fish, and again, pizza. But they are good also in marinades, in casseroles, in terrines and pâtés, but not, apparently, according to Erasmus, with pork – times have changed! I use marjoram as an all-rounder and I like

it with milky foods, yoghurts, cream dressings and cheeses. It is, or should be, one of the ingredients in a mixed bouquet garni. When dried, sweet or knotted marjoram is one of the constituents of 'sweet herbs' sold in packets.

Sweet or knotted marjoram is *Origanum marjorana*. This species is fairly tender and although it is a sub-shrub in the Mediterranean region it is usually treated as a half-hardy annual in colder countries. It will grow one to two feet tall. I find that it will grow rapidly on a sunny window-sill indoors and you can begin to pick it three months after sowing. Pot marjoram is *O. onites*, a perennial, 12 ins., which grows well outdoors in a warm, well drained light soil. Here it will form a good mat. Winter marjoram is *O. heracleoticum*, less hardy. Dittany of Crete is *O. dictamnus*. These can be increased by cuttings or divisions.

O. vulgare is the native European species. Its golden variety is described in the chapter on Herbs in the Modern Garden. It grows wild in some countries and I can never resist bringing home a bunch, for it gives casseroles a pungent, gamey flavour.

Rosemary

This is a herb which is fast coming back into favour. It is surprisingly versatile. It is especially good with all pale meats, a useful rule.

I like it particularly with veal and chicken. I have eaten it with goat and when meat was scarce and we lived off the land I always used it with squirrel. It improves rabbit and hare. Do try hare cooked in cider with rosemary. Lamb and mutton taste better with rosemary than with mint in my opinion.

Use it with vegetables, in pea, spinach and minestrone soups, the last with sage and tarragon added. Use it boiled with old potatoes. The leaves can be used to make tea and country wines. The flowers can be candied. Like several other culinary herbs it has other uses. (See Chapter four.)

The common rosemary, *Ros-*

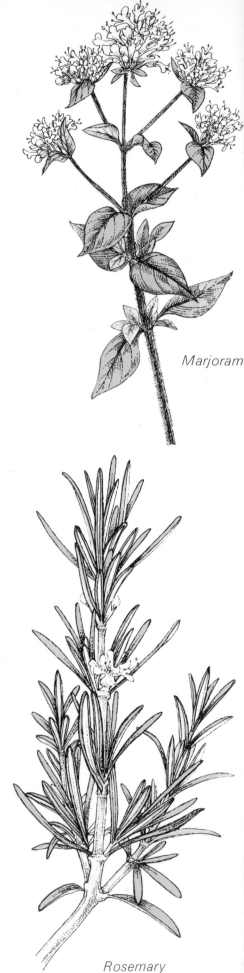

Marjoram

Rosemary

Sweet Marjoram

marinus officinalis, is an evergreen shrub which will grow as high as seven feet in spite of the legend that the plant never grows taller than Jesus Christ was when on earth. It is said also that when a plant reaches his earthly age, thirty years, it will grow no taller, only wider!

The flowers are a lovely blue and smother the stems in late spring. The more you cut rosemary the better, but this means taking only sprigs. If you cut it back hard into the old wood it is likely to die.

The plant thrives best in a light, dry soil in a sunny position and in spite of the fact that in Mediterranean regions it can be grown by the sea, in most countries it needs to be given a sheltered spot. Do not plant it in wet or heavy soils.

It can be raised from seed sown in spring in open soil but the best means of propagation is by six-inch long cuttings taken in summer and struck in sandy soil under a cloche or within a cold frame placed in a shady spot.

Savory

There are two kinds of savory, summer, *Satureia hortensis*, and winter, *S. montana*.

The first is an annual herb. It was noted by Virgil as among the most fragrant. See the section on dried herbs. It is good in pork pies, sausages, sauces for veal, pork and duck. Fresh sprigs can be boiled with young broad beans and peas in the same way as mint is used. It is a good herb for legumes, for it suits any beans, fresh or dried and all pulses. It is good with lentil soup, pease pudding and baked beans.

Rub savory on the spot if you are stung by a bee, for it is said to give relief. (I am not sure about a wasp sting.)

Winter savory can be used in the same way as summer, but it is not considered such a fragrant herb. It is a shrubby perennial and can be grown in districts where the summer kind may not do so well.

Sow the seed of summer savory in spring in the open ground where they are to grow. Thin them. They will sprout again after they are cut down.

Plants of winter savory can be divided in spring. Take side shoots, with a heel, for cuttings.

Balm

Many letters I receive from readers deal with this plant. The most frequent inquiry is simply, 'Can you eat it?' The answer is a definite 'Yes'.

Melissa officinalis is one of the herbs always to be found in my kitchen, for I include it in my daily posy during all but the very cold months, when it disappears. But even then a little can be forced.

The fresh leaves can be chopped and mixed in all kinds of dishes, salads, sauces and butters. I like to use them in chilled soups and in any dish where a little lemon flavour is needed. To all of these the herb is introduced only at the very last moment. It is not washed or chopped until it is required because it tends to become discoloured if prepared too far in advance. It is good with shellfish; try it chopped very finely in a moules mariniere bouillon. And if you like snails use plenty of melissa in the garlicky butter with which you stuff the shells. Country wines are made from it.

You will find more about balm in the chapter on Plants for Pot-Pourri.

It was used in the past for 'making a drink for sick persons'. It soothes the nerves, comforts the heart and drives away melancholy, qualities which should make it very popular today.

The leaves smell very strongly of lemon. Quite often you will

Savory

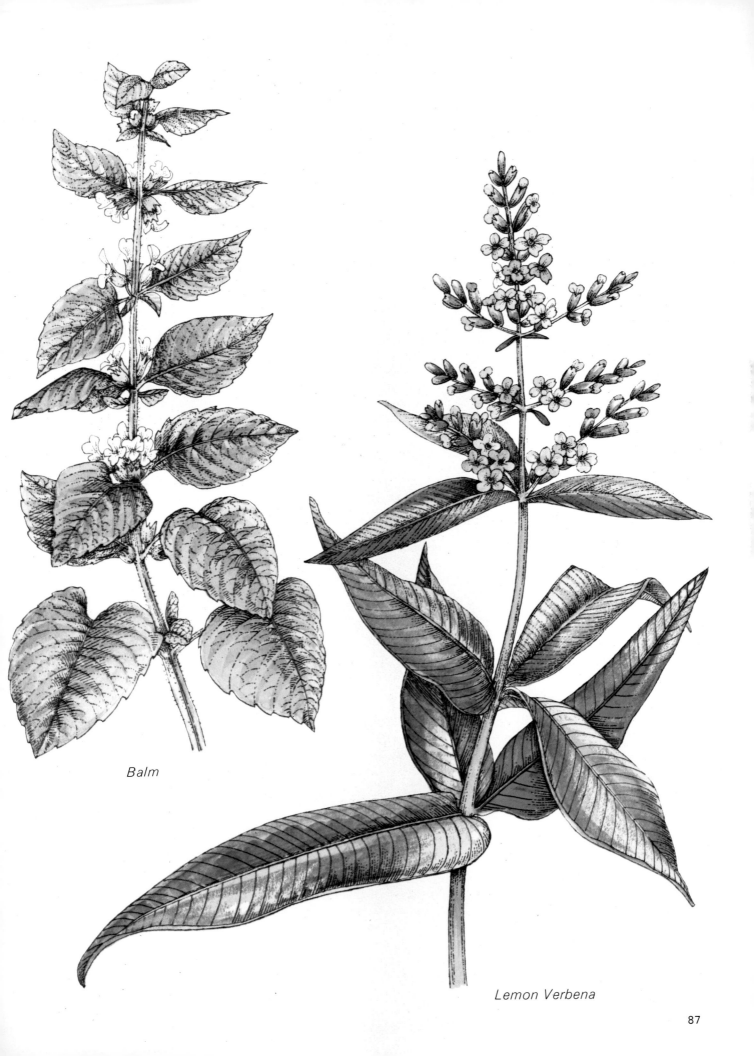

Balm

Lemon Verbena

87

Bergamot

find melissa called 'lemon verbena'. This is the name belonging
to a shrub *Lippia citriodora*, actually lemon-*scented* verbena. Some
other people call it lemon mint
and certainly sometimes the leaves
resemble mint in appearance. It is
also sometimes confused with
lemon thyme. But balm or melissa
is its proper name.

As the stems grow taller and
bloom, the leaves become tougher
and consequently not quite so
useful as when the shoots are
young. For this reason keep some
of the stems frequently cut so that
you have a supply of young leaves.

Melissa or balm is a hardy
perennial. Like mint it can be

invasive. It also seeds itself quite
vigorously so that there are times
when you must be quite ruthless
with it. It is advisable to lift old
plants every four years or so to
keep them under control.

The roots are mat-like and I find
them useful for binding the earth
of my herb bank. This means
though that a large plant can be
difficult to lift. This should be
done early in the autumn. Quite
small pieces of the root will grow
quickly into a good plant. I find
that the best way to divide a large
clump is to slice it through with a
spade, trim it by pulling away all
severed and loose growths, and
then replant.

For the lovely *Melissa officinalis
aurea*, the golden balm, see the
chapter on Herbs in the Modern
Garden.

Bergamot

There are two bergamots, one of
which is a mint, *Mentha citrata*,
which yields a fragrant lemon-
scented oil. You will find more
about this in the chapter on
Plants for Pot-Pourri.

What most of us mean by
bergamot is sweet bergamot, *Monarda didyma*. American readers
might like to know that the plant
is named in honour of Nicholas
Monardes, 1493 to 1588, who was a
Seville physician and botanist. In

Tarragon

1571, no doubt carried away by the wonderful discovery of a country across the globe, he wrote a book describing some of the American products. Translated into English it was called *Joyful News out of the New Found World*.

Obviously monarda and Oswego tea made from a brew of its leaves was one of these products. The leaves can be mixed with ordinary Indian tea to improve the flavour or make it go a little further. It can be used in salads, but only in moderation, for its pungency is a little sweet. It is a fine pot-pourri herb. *Monarda didyma* is easily grown in any ordinary soil, but this must not be

dry or the plants will not thrive.

There are many lovely varieties of this plant which will colour a herb garden prettily. Although the species seeds quite freely and well, the named hybrids should be increased by division in spring.

COMPOSITAE

Now we come to a completely different looking set of plants, members of the daisy tribe. As herbs they are few.

Tarragon

The most important is tarragon, *Artemisia dracunculus*, one of the many pungent artemisias. This really is a versatile herb and is

almost a necessity in some dishes. The blend of three herbs, chervil, chives and tarragon is thought by some gourmets to be perfect. It is the herb used in hollandaise, bearnaise and tartare sauces, or rather the herb which *should* be used. It is often made into a purée to flavour bechamel sauce for filling vol-au-vents and for serving with certain vegetables. It is made into butters to serve with vegetables and shell fish. A good chicken herb for either boiling or roasting, it is fine used with chicken livers; good also for fish, rabbit, veal and all egg dishes. It flavours vinegar. French mustard contains tarragon. It is good dried, when it becomes very aromatic. It is a bouquet garni herb.

There are two varieties, French tarragon with dark green smooth leaves and Russian tarragon from Siberia, the leaves of which are less smooth and the taste less tart. General opinion is that the French variety is best.

It is a hardy perennial except in severe winters when it should be given some protection. It grows roughly two feet in height, and prefers warm, dry soils. The plant can be increased by pulling the underground runners away and replanting them.

Plants force well in winter and for this purpose they can be lifted any time from autumn onwards, first having cut them back about a month earlier. They can be lifted and transplanted in frames or planted in ordinary soil in a box or large pot and grown in a warm greenhouse or in the home.

Alecost
This is also called Costmary, Sweet Mary, Allspice and Mace. The last two names are very confusing because they really belong to two completely different subjects. However, they give a clue to the flavour of this herb.

It is *Chrysanthemum balsamita*, once an important plant because its leaves were used to flavour ale.

They are also used in salads but are an acquired taste. Some people find them pleasant and for this reason I feel that the plant should be listed here. The leaves and shoots should be used very young.

I have often wondered why in American colonial days of all plants this should be chosen to mark the pages for the church service. For this reason it is known as Bible Leaf. Could it be, one wonders, that the pungent scent reminded those who opened the book at the right page of the Sunday meal and comforting drink awaiting them back home? Or does another name, Sweet Mary,

Alecost

Marigold

hold a religious clue?

It is a hardy perennial, tall, reaching as much as five feet in some cases, with yellow button flowers. It likes a warm, well drained situation.

Marigold

One should always be sure to add the term 'pot' to the name. There are many marigolds and only one for the pot, *Calendula officinalis*.

I remember first reading about it as a culinary herb in a description by some traveller of former times, reporting that in 'Dutchland' they were to be seen on sale by the barrelful for the flavouring of soups.

Like the camomile, its near relative, the pot marigold is grown for its flowers. These are sometimes used as a substitute or as an adulterant for the more expensive saffron, so try them in buns or with rice.

Those who are interested in the visual appeal of food should consider using them as a garnish. A birthday or party cake for children freshly decorated with a ring of marigolds looks charming, a real delight dish!

Only the outer ray florets are used. There is more information on this plant in the chapter on Drying Herbs. The petals can be included in pot-pourri for their

colour value as well as their pungent scent. It is because of their colour that I am so pleased to know that they are a wholesome herb. The bright orange is a perfect colour to complement the blues and purples of many herb flowers, and to brighten the greys and greens of the herb border.

Since they are hardy annuals the seeds can be sown either in autumn or in spring. They flower all summer long. They should be frequently picked if the flowering season is to be a long one. They will seed themselves freely.

Camomile

One wonders at what point we

Camomile

stopped being so dependent upon camomile. Was it when aspirin became more used? *Anthemis nobilis* was once highly valued as a febrifuge and it was consumed mightily as a tonic. All that is left now is camomile tea, a pleasant tisane which many find soothing and comforting.

The herb is listed here simply because it is such a good tea plant and also because I think it is always useful for the imaginative cook to know what flowers are wholesome. These little daisies can also be used for party food decoration.

The flowers were once used in the toilette, being especially recommended as a hair rinse for those with blond hair.

It is a perennial herb best grown in fairly dry, light but rich soil.

More information appears in the chapters on Drying Herbs and Herbs for the Modern Garden.

LILIACEAE
Garlic

Once you have used garlic, *Allium sativum*, in your cooking you will find that many dishes seem insipid without it. I find many people are prejudiced against it without ever having knowingly tasted this valuable herb. Indeed, there have been times when they have sat at my table eating a dish with garlic in it and have told me quite solemnly that garlic was just one thing that they could never bring themselves to eat, meanwhile clearing their plates attentively. If you have never tried garlic please do! I cannot imagine how I ever cooked without it. It would never have been praised and used as an essential ingredient for all these centuries if it had not been tried and found good.

A word of caution. If you are going to use garlic use it properly. Some people like to include a clove of garlic in a dish at the last moment. If you do this, don't forget to take it out. Taking one soft, freshly-cooked clove in one's mouth is very different from merely eating a dish which has been garlic flavoured.

I have much more to say about garlic in the Recipe Chapter.

This useful pungent vegetable is often expensive to buy, but it really is cheap and easy to grow. If you have no garden you can grow garlic in deep pots.

Divide the compound bulb into separate cloves and plant them two inches deep and four to six inches apart from late winter to spring. One clove produces a compound bulb.

Lift the bulbs when they are ripe. By this time the green tops will have faded. Spread them out on the ground and let them dry a little in the air first and then hang them in a dry, cool place in ropes or loose in nets.

The bulbs are hardy. For early crops plant some cloves in autumn from the freshly lifted bulbs.

If you are short of chives or any other green onion top, you can safely cut garlic foliage to use instead. And if you have used your store of dried bulbs, the freshly pulled bulbs can be used. This is a little extravagant perhaps, but better than going without.

Shallots

It is claimed by some that what gives French cooking its special taste is not so much the garlic but rather the shallots which are so frequently used. Certainly these do give a fine tang to flavours, nuttier than an onion and distinct from garlic. I would say that no aspiring cook should be without shallots. And they are so easy to grow. Like garlic, one small bulb taken from a cluster will produce many. They can be grown in rows across a vegetable garden, down the side of a sunny path, or perhaps hidden away behind a row of flowers or in groups in a herb border if there is no room for them elsewhere.

Shallots, *Allium ascalonicum*, are not raised from packeted seed but from individual bulbs known as 'seed'. If you cannot get them from a seed merchant, those you

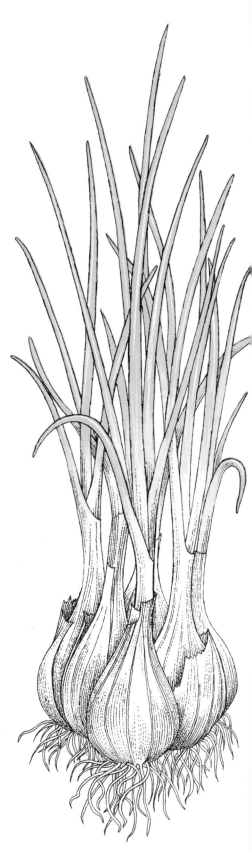

Shallots

Garlic

buy from the delicatessen or greengrocer will do as well. Plant them six inches apart in rows a foot apart. You can plant them really early (some say on the shortest day) but I usually plant mine in late spring.

Make a small depression in the soil with a trowel, plant the bulb and cover it almost to the top. If you plant them the way most often recommended by just pressing the bulbs into the soil leaving the bulk above soil level you will find that worms will soon push the bulbs out of place. Later, when they have rooted and begun

to shoot, you can move the soil away from them again.

Wait until the leaves fade completely before you harvest the bulbs, although of course you can pull them while they are still green if you so wish, in which case use the green tops as well as the bulb. Let the shallots dry in the air a little and store them the same way as garlic.

After I lift mine, and especially if the season has been a wet one, I lay them on a piece of plastic sheeting under a cloche with open sides until the skins feel dry and papery.

There are two kinds of shallots, those with yellow and those with red skins. The first are less strong in flavour but they keep better during the winter.

Chives
Here's a useful herb, one of the fines herbes and one that you can have at hand even if you have no garden. You can use chives in so many dishes, in soups and sauces, especially in the creamy kinds and essentially in vichyssoise; in cream cheese, omelettes, custards, with jacket potatoes, mainly as a garnish, sometimes as a con-

Chives

diment and sometimes cooked, but always just at the very last moment otherwise they lose their good colour.

These really are cut and come again plants. One begins to cut the 'grass' as soon as it is long enough to hold properly. One should not denude the whole plant at one time, so take a small bunch from each plant if you need a quantity. This is one reason why these are good herbs to have in a row, so that one plant can be recovering while another is being harvested. Gather the bunch, tie it in the centre to keep the stems under control and snip the leaves across into fine sections either with scissors or with a sharp knife. The bunch will keep fresh in water for a day or two but is better kept out of water in a covered container in a refrigerator.

Chives are hardy perennials and are easily grown in any ordinary good soil. They should be divided after three or four years. Simply lift the roots in spring or autumn and pull them apart. You will see that they are really bunches of tiny onions. Replant small clusters.

I have found that the seed germinates extremely well on a warm window-sill and if no greenhouse is available this is a good means of keeping a supply going throughout the winter. Sow several pots at different times to give a succession.

Chive flowers are very pretty. If you have a row of plants arrange them so that they flower alternately.

INDIVIDUAL HERBS
Some of the herbs we use are the only culinary member of their families, so I now deal with these in alphabetical order. It so happens, however, that the first in the list is also the top of the list for its herb value. This is bay, *Laurus nobilis*.

Bay
First a word of caution. This is the only true laurel although the

Bay

name is applied to some members of the prunus genus. The other so-called laurels are not wholesome and should not be used in cooking.

Almost all savoury dishes are improved by the addition of bay. Usually one leaf or a pinch of dried and powdered leaf is sufficient. Bay is an essential ingredient of a bouquet garni. It is also used in pot-pourri.

Bay trees are seldom cheap because they take so long to mature, but the bay can be propagated by taking cuttings of three to four inch long shoots of half-ripened stems from the end of summer to early autumn. Strike them like most others, in sandy soil under a cloche in a shady place outdoors. Shoots may also be layered. Put the layers in place in the autumn.

Bays love to be grown in sunshine and protected from cold winds.

Borage

Borage, *Borago officinalis*, is a delightful plant some two to three feet tall and beginning to flower at an early stage. It has an attractive summer-haze appearance as it begins to age. Sprigs, including flower stems, are used in claret and other wine cups and fruit drinks of all kinds. Young leaves can be used in salads cooked like spinach, or dipped in batter as fritters. The lovely blue flowers may be candied for cake decorations. Gather these just before they open so that they keep their colour. The plant is much visited by bees.

It is a hardy annual that will grow in ordinary soils. Sow seed in spring for summer flowering or in autumn for spring. Once grown, plants usually seed themselves.

Horse-radish

With horse-radish, *Cochlearia armoracia*, the root only is used and the outer part is the strongest flavoured. The grated root is used in sauces for smoked fish, beef and salad dressings.

Borage

Horse-radish

The plant is a hardy perennial with large leaves and it grows some two feet tall. It is best grown in a piece of land apart from other plants because it can be so invasive. For a regular supply replant pieces of root 18 ins. apart each winter. Make root cuttings by dividing a root into two or three-inch lengths. Dibble these into the soil so that they lie about four inches under the surface.

Juniper berries

Since I first gathered my own juniper berries, *Juniperus communis*, while on holiday in France and brought them back to use in my cooking this herb has become more and more important to me. The berries – botanically really cones – can be added, first pounded, to marinades and to stews. Their flavour is not dominating. Five or six berries are usually sufficient for the average dish.

The plant, a shrub which belongs to the pinaceae, grows low and spreading or tall and erect according to its environment and the condition of the soil. This species has given rise to many garden varieties.

Nasturtium

The leaves of nasturtium, *Tropaeolum majus*, have a sharp, cress-like flavour and the flower buds are less strongly flavoured. Both can be mixed in salads. They are also good in sandwiches.

The fat young seeds are crisper and stronger than the leaves. They can be chopped and used in many ways. They are particularly good used in a sauce tartare and as a substitute for horse-radish. They can also be pickled in vinegar, like shallots, when they are known as false capers.

The plant will grow in almost any soil. The poorer it is the more flowers you can expect, a point to bear in mind if you are raising the plants to eat. The seeds should be sown, singly, in late spring.

Juniper Berries   *Nasturtium*

Dried Herbs

Most herbs which are to be dried should be cut on a dry and sunny day. Use scissors or secateurs rather than attempt to pick them with your fingers. You want the stems to come clean and not with pieces of root adhering, for you do not want to collect soil as well. Gather tips rather than the full stem. Often after you have picked a crop like this side shoots will develop to give you a new harvest later in the summer and autumn.

Divide the shoots into small bunches, small so that the air can circulate. Put each kind in its own bunch, except of course for any bouquet garni that you may make. Cut off dead and imperfect leaves before drying the stems.

If the herbs are likely to be dusty, wash them thoroughly in clean cold water and shake them dry.

Much has been written about drying herbs and it seems to me that this process is often unnecessarily involved and complicated. The best way of drying just a few herbs, say the remains of an extra generous handful you may have picked, is to put them inside a large brandy balloon type glass and to stand this in a sunny

Left: A beautiful herbal flower arrangement can be made from fresh herbs picked from the garden in summer. During winter or towards the end of summer *they can be used for drying for cooking. All the herbs pictured can be dried for cooking, except rue, the tall blue one in the centre.* *This page top: The male flowers of bay,* Laurus nobilis. *Left: An attractive herb border in early June. Right: A useful jar of dried bay leaves.*

window until they are dry, usually two or three days; a very simple process. Of course there is a great difference between handling the residue of a bunch and a large crop gathered from many plants.

Methods used for drying herbs include: hanging bunches outdoors in half shade during the warmest part of the day for several days; hanging them in a warm kitchen away from steam, putting small bunches in open plastic bags and simply leaving them hanging in a warm dry place in the kitchen until they are needed;

stringing them on sticks and/or hanging them from oven racks; placing them on the racks, in which case they must be turned frequently; hanging or spreading them on paper in an airing cupboard.

Whatever method you use remember that herbs dried away from direct sunlight keep their colour best. You will find that some dry faster than others. Some herbs take several weeks to become really dry. Even when they feel dry to the touch it is well to make sure that they really are quite free from moisture. Untie the bunches, spread the sprigs on

oven foil and dry for ten minutes, no more, in a pre-heated oven at 200°F. Give sage three minutes longer than this.

Do bear in mind that too much heat dries out essential oils. Herbs which retain their colour will also retain their oils and their fragrance. Succulent herbs such as mints, parsley and fennel can be spread thinly on paper to dry in the warm air or in a warm oven. When the leaves are dry to the touch the bunches may be placed in paper or plastic bags, closed tightly at the mouth and stored in a dry place just as they are.

However, if you want to powder the herbs, strip the leaves from the stems and rub them

through your hands. If they are properly dried they should powder easily. If you want the powder to be really fine, as with bay leaves for instance, use an electric coffee grinder. It is possible to kill smells before using it again for coffee by wiping the container around with the remains of a squeezed lemon

or with a tissue on which a few drops of lemon juice have been squeezed.

Those who dislike herbs often criticise them by remarking that they are indigestible, and if you pursue the matter further you will almost certainly find the herbs in question have been dried. Instead of soothing the stomach, which after all is the true use of the herb, dried herbs used too generously unfortunately have the opposite effect.

One must remember that when leaves are dried the essential herbs are contained in much smaller bulk than they are in the fresh leaf. Often only a pinch of dried herbs is required to give the desired flavour, yet in the same dish you could probably use the fresh herbs over-generously and still find it enjoyable and easily digested.

It is best always to begin by adding very little, allowing the dish to absorb the flavour, then taste again and adjust the flavouring, adding a little more at this stage should this appear necessary. In time experience will guide the cook.

In my opinion it is best to use fresh herbs wherever possible. I use them the year round, lifting, protecting and forcing them according to the kind. I seldom use dried herbs, except bay.

Most culinary herbs retain their pungency when dried, but there are some which are not worth drying. Examples are chives, borage, balm and chervil. The others should be harvested just before they come into full bloom, for it is at this time that they are most pungent and contain the greatest amount of the essential oils in which their flavours are held.

*A simple drying.
technique for pot-pourri*

In old recipes for pot-pourri one is often told to gather the petals and then spread them on paper or linen out of doors in the shade. This is often a hazardous and painstaking task! Ideal, no doubt, where no winds blow and the weather is always clement and if conditions are ideal for you then by all means follow this method. However, here is a simpler one. Collect or buy the net bags used for packing oranges, apples and other foods in the supermarkets. These are of various sized meshes and you can always find one suitable for the flowers or leaves you wish to dry. Pack the materials in quite loosely, for you will find the level will fall as they dry, and hang them in some cool, airy place. If they wave around in the wind so much the better. From time to time tip them into another sack so that the top goes to the bottom. Once they feel dry spread them out indoors.

Cooking with Herbs

When I used to divide my time between town and country, the freshly gathered fruit and vegetables we brought back to the city made the tedious journeys all worth while. But there were often times when for one reason or another none could be gathered. Then I compromised by quickly collecting a large bunch of mixed fresh herbs, for I knew by experience that these would bring country flavour to market-worn and highly processed town foods.

Fresh herbs can be used liberally to transform mundane foods. Ta e frozen plaice or flounder fillets for instance, a marvellous standby for the busy cook. It should first be placed in a buttered oven dish, dotted with butter, seasoned, honoured with a sprig of fresh thyme, covered with foil, and baked in a moderate oven for twenty-five minutes or so. Then it can be taken out, covered with hot cream and well garnished with either chopped green chervil or fennel or perhaps, for an intriguing change, a little sweet cicely. Meanwhile, the frozen peas can be cooked in a little salted water with three or four chopped young shallots, green tops and all (this

Left: Jacket potatoes served with herb butter. Chives, parsley and fennel are on the board; parsley, thyme, fennel, sage, mint, rosemary and bay in the background.

Above: A dish of plaice to give you an appetite. The plaice are cooked with thyme and served with hot cream garnished with fennel.

makes them both sweet and tender), and a sprig or two of fresh mint to give them a real garden flavour.

Frozen vegetables are good value but they tend to pall when eaten regularly. Ring the changes with herbs. Try chopped mint on peas instead of cooking it with them. Another time, shred the outer leaves of lettuce to cook with them and garnish the strained mixture with finely chopped parsley and raw spring onion or scallion tops or with chives.

Use fresh basil with beans or, alternatively, that much abused herb, sage. This is a deliciously pungent herb which can be used fresh for every kind of bean, fresh, frozen, canned and dried, home-grown or imported. Chop the sage really fine and use it discreetly, for it is very full flavoured. Begin with a little and add to it.

Herb butters bring a new flavour to chops, frozen hamburgers, sausages, grilled (broiled) fish, jacket-baked potatoes or even the instant mash. Use a heaped teaspoon, at least, of finely chopped herbs, either of one kind or mixed (try marjoram with beef), to two ounces of butter or margarine. Just blend them together with a palette knife. Place a knob of herb butter on the dish as you serve it.

Mixed herbs make easy yet savoury salad dressings. Mix them into natural yoghurt, double cream, mayonnaise. Grate odds and ends of dry cheese, as mixed as you like, cream them by adding milk or yoghurt and add herbs to make an economical cream cheese or a cracker dip.

You can introduce summer radishes into any of these mixtures. Mix them with walnuts,

both coarsely chopped and liberally laced with chives, in cream or cottage cheese. Serve mixed herbs with summer soups, hot or chilled, and vary these by adding finely chopped radish.

Fines herbes for omelettes is a blend of parsley, chervil, tarragon and chives. Try these on scrambled eggs and baked eggs also. Use them with cream, even canned, and with yoghurt to cover hard-boiled eggs. Vary all kinds of egg dishes, soufflés, baked savoury custards, oeufs en cocotte, with this mixture.

Change the concept and the taste of frozen chicken and turkey by using rosemary, tarragon or even lavender. If you broil or grill them, tie the sprigs on each side of the bird. For roasting, chop the herb and sprinkle it over the breast with a little salt. Just before taking it finally from the oven, say ten minutes beforehand, squeeze a lemon over the skin and use more lemon juice to remove the brown juices from the pan before adding stock for gravy. Boil any roasted pieces of herb with this. Strain before serving. Use tarragon with boiling fowl and thus make marvellous stock.

I wouldn't think of cooking meat in any way without some herb to go with it. Simple traditional roasts can be given extra flavour. A small sprig of rosemary, scattered leaf by leaf over a shoulder or best end of neck of

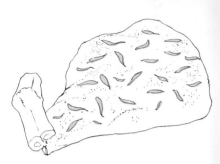

lamb, will give the meat a delicious aroma while cooking and a special taste when it is eaten. You could strew finely chopped garlic over the surface as well.

Some cooks like to use slivers of garlic and to push them into the surface of joints of veal. Veal tasting as it so often does today, I prefer to marinate it, using garlic,

shallots, rosemary and bay in the wine and oil mixture. The same goes for the cheaper joints of beef, although for these I use marjoram

and thyme instead of rosemary and from time to time add juniper berries. When I fry veal chops or escallopes of veal, I also fry a little rosemary in the butter. But-

Quantities of ingredients for the recipes in this section have been measured according to the following table.

1 cup=½ pint or 8 tablespoons

1 tablespoon=3 teaspoons

ter for beef steaks is savoured by frying chopped garlic and shallot in it first.

Pork is more tender and tastes better if you first smear mustard over the surface and sprinkle a

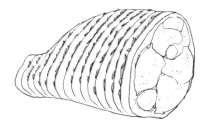

little fresh chopped sage on the skin or down between the cuts if this has been scored. Sage is also good sprinkled on other 'fat' meats such as goose and duck. It is often worth while to remake sausages by adding chopped sage to them.

Baked and grilled (broiled) fish improves with thyme and fennel. You can grill fish on fennel stalks which gives it a delicious flavour. Try this when you hold a barbecue sometime. Mackerel are especially good.

Yet while I may roast-garnish meat and fish with a variety of herbs I am careful not to use thyme this way. I have already said that this is an all-rounder, one of our most important herbs, but it should be used inside meats rather than outside them; in stuffings, stews, and, in my opinion, only in baked meats and fish where these are covered. Roasting

seems to accentuate its already dominant flavour.

When canned vegetables are used, see that they are always brought to life with a fresh herb garnish. Sprinkle basil on tomatoes (on fresh ones as well!), chervil on celery, parsley on carrots and mint, chives, or borage on potatoes. For a change, use fennel or winter savory where hitherto you have used mint.

Some of the most simple and

filling foods can be transformed by using herbs. Take spaghetti for instance; after cooking, drain, return to the pan, add butter and have ready a good quantity of very finely chopped herbs which should contain some basil. Sprinkle these on the pasta. Take two large forks (I use a carving fork and the large kitchen fork) and lift high above the rim of the pan, turning it as you tease the spaghetti so that each strand is unbroken but covered with the butter and the herbs. This makes a good and unusual first course.

Obviously, the same can be done with any other pasta. If you have cooked too much spaghetti at any time, while it is still warm,

repeat this process, this time using French dressing instead of butter. It will keep in the refrigerator for 48 hours once dressed.

Rice and herbs, whether plain boiled, risotto or creamed, is also good and needs less expensive foods to accompany it, should you be operating on a strict budget.

If you have a young and hungry family to feed, serve a batter or Yorkshire pudding more frequently than with roast beef. Savour this in various ways, using garlic, shallots and herbs, either in mixtures or of one kind. For a sweet, make the same pudding offered with chopped mint and plenty of sugar or syrup.

Sprinkle rosemary on fried potatoes. Fry parsnips like French fries and garnish them with fried parsley.

To get the full value from any herbs you grow, get into the habit of using them! One of the best ways of ensuring that you have plenty near to hand is to bring in a good posy of them each evening after you have looked round the garden. Stand the posy in water on the window-sill in good light but not in full sunshine in case the stems wilt. If you grow herbs in containers you can arrange to have a supply near at hand, growing but not cut.

If you have to depend upon a gift bunch of herbs divide the bunch and keep half in water on the sill and store the remainder in the refrigerator. Make sure that they are dry, but not dried! Simply pat them with a piece of paper towel if the leaves seem to be moist. Store them in a covered plastic box and put them at the bottom of the refrigerator.

Alternatively, keep them in the freezer. Many of the leafy herbs can be successfully stored this

Marinated steak (page 116): This steak with shelled bean salad (page 113) has a dish of tomatoes baked with herbs to go with it, as well as pickled shallots in the jar, and French dressing in the jug. The herbs in the background, from the left, are sage, dill, chervil and chives. Winter savory, dill and tarragon are in front of the tomatoes. On the right, from the back, are balm, bay, marjoram and shallots. Balm is also in front: horse-radish is being grated on the left.

way. Wash and dry them well, taking care that you do not bruise the leaves. Place small amounts in small packages, plastic bags or cartons, or in cooking oil. When you are ready to use them either toss them into the cooking vegetables, mint into peas for example, or for sauces shave them while they are still frozen. A friend of mine 'puts up' a number of cartons of mint and sugar ready for mint sauce. The two are chopped together, then frozen. To make the sauce, the vinegar is simply poured over the frozen mixture and left to thaw.

The longer that herbs are left in a freezer, the greater the loss of flavour.

Almost every dish you prepare can be enriched by herbs. For instance, try fresh chopped herbs on cold meat in a sandwich or sprinkle a little chives on toasted cheese.

Do not tie the Cordon Bleu ribbon to herbs. Remember that they have long belonged in the most basic of foods, not the most sophisticated. Think of them as a means to help you to vary and stretch simple foods as well as to create memorable dishes. One of my specialities is a summer chilled soup made with a white stock, mixed with cream, canned if necessary, (unexpected guests are often served with this particular dish) well laced with garlic and lemon and finally 'greened' with finely chopped herbs. These are added just before serving but the garlic is added in the early preparation of the stock. Sometimes I stir in a little curry powder. The soup always varies a little because it depends on what ingredients are at hand. If, for instance, I have cooked vegetables, including any kind of green vegetable, the water

from these is saved and used instead of, or blended with, the stock. The cream thickens the soup. If I want it thicker I might add a puréed potato or a well beaten egg. I like to use a little diced cucumber sometimes but failing this I add more chopped borage or salad burnet than usual.

This makes a very inexpensive course for six or more people, yet it never savours of penny pinching. Surely, if there is good food at hand such as stock or vegetable water it is a waste of time and material not to use it, and herbs help to present it in an appetising way. Once when a guest was praising this particular soup and asked for more, and how it was made, I tried to explain my attitude to cooking, but was unable to do so. His interruption delighted me. 'Just forget the philosophy,' he told me, 'and pass on the recipe!'

At this point I propose to take his advice and have the pleasure of sharing some of my favourite recipes. Many of them are, as far as I know, original, though this is a claim I am hesitant to make because other herb-happy cooks may have created similar dishes. Read them, try them and, please, experiment as I have done.

In the main, the recipes come under the heading of the herbs used in them rather than under one which defines the nature of the dish. I begin with dishes in which mainly mixed herbs are used. First though, a few definitions, to guide the new cook.

Bouquet Garni is a little bunch or bouquet, small, medium or 'large', tied in a muslin bag when dried and when fresh often tied with a long thread to facilitate easy removal from the pot. It is used to flavour sauces, stews,

while cooking. Also used in marinades. The basic herbs are parsley, thyme, bay. Stronger and more aromatic herbs are often used in marinades. Sometimes parsley alone is used as a bouquet garni. There is no hard and fast rule, e.g. a court bouillon often needs a strong bouquet and in cooked marinades one often includes parsley roots, celery, fennel, thyme, bay, coriander seeds, peppercorns, all boiled together for 20 minutes.
Herb juices are used to flavour and colour sauces. They are made from watercress (which provides a good colour), chervil, parsley, tarragon, pounded in a mortar and strained.
Marinade Herbs, a bouquet garni slightly stronger than that used in actual cooking. Essential are parsley, thyme and bay but other herbs are added according to the dish and to personal taste.
Turtle Herbs are basil, marjoram, sorrel and thyme. These are used to flavour soups or sauces *a la tortue*.
Pot Herbs. This term does not really apply to flavouring herbs but to those herbs or plants which are used in the preparation of soups. They are mostly orach, spinach, lettuce, sorrel, seakale, and purslane, in French cooking. In this country the term is usually applied to roots only which are used in soups and stews, carrots, turnips, parsnips and celery.
Remoulade, is a mayonnaise to which is added parsley, spring onions or scallions, chervil, tarragon, gherkins, capers, all finely chopped together and mixed with anchovy essence (or extract).
Escoffier mayonnaise, considered especially good with cold beef, is made by mixing to the sauce grated horse-radish, chopped parsley and chopped chervil.

Sweet Herbs. The term does not really apply to taste. Some sweet herbs are, in fact, very bitter and are not used in cooking. This is the old name given to those used, or once used, in pot-pourris, cosmetics, sachets, scents, washing waters; as prophylactics and antiseptics; for strewing on the floors; as love philtres and potions and for some confectionery.

Condiments are aromatic substances (with the exception of salt), mostly of vegetable matter, added to food to improve its flavour after the food has been cooked or at table. Fresh herbs rather than dried are used in this respect.

Seasonings are substances, particularly salt, added to foods during cooking to improve taste rather than flavour. Herbs are not strictly seasonings although many spices are.

Herb vinegars. You can flavour vinegars with various herbs to give extra taste to salad dressings and sauces. These are best made with either cider or wine vinegars. I use home-made-wine vinegar. The basic recipe is

Tarragon vinegar. Take one pint of leaves to 1½ pints of vinegar. Place the leaves in a jar and pour

the vinegar on them. Cover the jar to keep the contents airtight. Leave for a week. Strain off the vinegar and bottle.

This makes a good aromatic vinegar. The same method can be used for other herbs such as rosemary and thyme.

Garlic vinegar

6 large or 8 medium sized garlic cloves
salt
1 pint vinegar

Pound the garlic. Boil the vinegar and pour it over the garlic placed in a warmed jar. Cool it and cover. Let the garlic steep for two or three weeks then strain and bottle it.

Garlic is so important to my kind of cooking that not only do I grow a long row across my kitchen garden but I also bring back ropes of the great clustered cloves from France whenever I visit that country. I know that many people say that you should only bruise, grate or squeeze garlic, but I usually prefer to chop it very, very fine. When I mix it with onion and shallot and 'melt' the three in butter or olive oil, the garlic pieces seem to disappear altogether, leaving just the flavour.

Garlic is deliciously nutty, when finely sliced and browned in butter until it is crisp. My family like it this way with liver – one or two small cloves is enough for a pound of the meat.

Equally important are shallots. These give a special taste, the real French flavour to food. Although onions are more bulky and often essential for certain dishes, I would rather be without them than without shallots. Fortunately, these store well.

I begin many dishes by melting

garlic, shallot and onion. Make a special white sauce this way. Take a tablespoon of chopped onion, one chopped clove of garlic, and a dessertspoon of chopped shallot. Gently melt them in an ounce of butter in a covered pan. When all are transparent but not brown, stir in a tablespoon of plain flour. You can vary the sauce by sometimes using wholemeal or wholewheat flour.

Take the pan off the heat and blend all together. Return to the heat, add a half pint of milk, stirring it all the time.

You can use this as a base for all kinds of other dishes. For instance, add a small can of shrimps to it and pour the sauce over halved hard-boiled eggs arranged in a shallow oven dish. Sprinkle with cheese and a dash of nutmeg and brown under the grill (broiler). For the young, for a quick snack, stir in a can of salmon and heap the thick sauce on toast, and garnish with chopped parsley or fennel.

This sauce is also the basis of a quick, good, soup. Simply add the water vegetables have been boiled in, a little cream and chopped herbs.

Shallot butter

Used for hors d'oeuvres and sandwiches is very good. Bring three ounces of shallots to the boil in very little water. Remove, cool them under cold water, drain and pound them to a pulp. Add an equal amount of butter. Blend the two together well. Use this for spreading on toast, bread, biscuits, crackers. To use for garnishing grills, simply add finely chopped parsley or any other herb you fancy.

Grilled mackerel (page 105): and
how tempting it looks! Chives are
sprinkled in the summer chilled
soup; also shown are thyme,
mackerel cooked on fennel stalks,
and parsley. A few shallots and
some herb bread made with shallot
butter complete the picture and a
delicious meal.

Pickled Shallots

The best kind of pickled onions! I use mine mostly to incorporate in varied salad creams or mayonnaises and salad dressings. Try one or two chopped and mixed with apple, radish and mixed herbs in yoghurt.

It is important that the shallots remain crisp so boil the spices in the vinegar, allow this to cool thoroughly before pouring it over the shallots.

To each quart of shallots you need

1 quart vinegar
½ oz pickling spice
¼ oz cloves
¼ oz peppercorns
2 bay leaves
2 ozs sugar

Peel the shallots, sprinkle them with 1½ ozs of salt and let them stand all night. Rinse them under the cold tap to remove the salt. Drain and dry them. Pack them into jars, leaving enough headroom for the vinegar to cover them completely. Tap the jars from time to time as you fill them so that the shallots settle and make more space for others.

Tie down or cover securely. Do not let the metal tops come in contact with the vinegar. These are ready for eating in two or three months.

Having introduced you to both these members of the onion family and explained their importance, we can now move on to other foods. And since I find a few basic dishes so helpful let me elaborate on one which is of great value both to those who like herbs and who like to budget carefully.

Baked savoury custards

If you are of an experimental turn of mind, here is a little department of cooking where you can play to your heart's content. The basic ingredients are those for a baked egg custard but instead of sugar one adds salt. This really is a simple recipe and I recommend it warmly to the busy ones because the dish can be prepared so well in advance and cooked without fuss.

The simplest of all variations is as follows:

¾ pint of milk
2 large eggs or 3 standard eggs
salt, pepper,
mixed chopped herbs,
nutmeg

This makes a simple first course which can be served hot or cold.

Beat the eggs and add to the milk. If you like garlic flavour, crush a clove, let it steep in this mixture for a while and remove it before cooking. Add salt and pepper to taste. Have the herbs ready, be sure to include some chives. Divide the milk and egg mixture between the six dishes. Add the herbs to each, the tops should be covered with a green 'mat'. Sprinkle nutmeg over the herbs.

Place the dishes in a baking tin. They should not touch each other. Pour in water to reach just below the rims of the dishes. Bake at 275°F. (135°C.) gas mark ½, for about an hour or until a crust appears on top of the custards and you can see that they have set. Too great a heat may curdle them.

Serves 6.

This mixture gives a fairly bland custard but you can vary it considerably to suit your own tastes. Many other ingredients can be added to the milk and egg.

I like them cooked with fish – for a special treat use the cheaper forms of caviare. I often divide a small can of shrimps or tuna between the six dishes. In this case I use chervil or fennel for the herb with a good pinch of cumin seed. When I use the liquor from canned foods, I measure it and subtract the amount from the amount of milk used.

Chopped mushroom, cheese, minced chicken, cooked vegetables, minced cooked ham or precooked chopped bacon served with a little sage are all delicious. The spices also can play a role here. Poppy seeds and caraway seeds, used separately, of course, impart an unusual flavour to the custards. If you like your food well seasoned use curry, paprika and a dash of Worcester sauce.

Marigold custard

You can also make a very unusual sweet herby custard using sugar, marigold petals and vanilla in the egg and milk. Use equal quantities of petals and milk. Pound the petals in a mortar. Blend all together and divide into separate dishes. Serve each one garnished with a whole flower or a mixture of petals and borage flowers.

And now for a few individual dishes.

Summer Dip

2 cartons or 6 ozs cottage cheese
1 cup cucumber peeled and diced
¼ cup chives
¼ cup parsley
1 tablespoon salad burnet
1 tablespoon borage
¼ cup chopped radish or
1 tablespoon horse-radish

Blend these ingredients together, making sure that the herbs are chopped finely. Chill the dip a little before serving. Garnish with borage flowers and nasturtium buds. If the dip needs to be a little more liquid you can add lemon juice, milk or even a little dry sherry.

This is a basic recipe on which you can play many variations according to what ingredients you have at hand. Other ingredients that suit the dip are chopped nuts of all kinds including salted peanuts, chopped dill pickles, nasturtium seeds or shredded nasturtium leaves, chopped ends of thick watercress stalks, and radish seeds – take these fresh from the swollen pods of plants which have run to seed.

Party dish.

Tomatoes baked with herbs

4 large tomatoes
1 tablespoon finely chopped or minced onion
1 tablespoon chopped fresh basil
1 tablespoon fresh dill
1 teaspoon celery seed
½ cup coarse dried white breadcrumbs
1 oz butter
salt and pepper

Cut the tomatoes in half round their 'equators'. Do not peel, and if you have to pull off the stems do not tear the flesh. Place them cut side uppermost in a shallow oven dish. Season. Mix the onions and herbs and sprinkle the mixture over the tomatoes. Top this with the breadcrumbs and dot these with the butter. Bake at 400°F. (204°C.), gas mark 6 for 15 mins.

This is good served with rice.
Serves 4.

Shelled Bean Salad

I quart of any freshly shelled beans you may have grown or can buy. (Canned shelled beans can be used for this recipe, in which case simply drain them and follow the recipe after directions about boiling the raw beans.)

2 small green onions
1 shallot with green top
b.g. of thyme, sage, bay leaf tied with onion and shallot greens
French dressing
2 tablespoons mixed chopped chives, chervil and parsley

Boil the beans putting them in boiling water with the b.g., the shallot and one of the onions. Slice the other finely. When the beans are tender, in about 15 minutes, drain the beans, remove the herbs. While the beans are still warm, mix them with the sliced onion, the chopped herbs and the dressing.

Taste, add freshly milled pepper to suit your palate. Allow to cool. Serve on crisp lettuce leaves.
Serves 4.

Lamb and aubergine casserole
(page 116): A spread to feast your
friends with. The main dish is
accompanied by peas cooked
French style and fish paté
flavoured with dill. Garlic,

shallots, rosemary, chervil,
fennel, peppercorns and cloves
are on the board. Thyme is
in the centre foreground and
parsley and bay in the background.

Lamb and Aubergine (eggplant) casserole

3 cups of pared and diced
aubergine (eggplant)
2 cups tomatoes peeled and
sliced
2 tablespoons finely chopped or
minced onion
1 clove garlic finely chopped
2 cups cooked lamb diced
2 tablespoons olive oil
2 tablespoons chopped parsley
½ teaspoon fresh rosemary
sprig of thyme
bay leaf
1 teaspoon salt
¼ teaspoon pepper
4 black olives sliced (and stoned,
of course)
½ cup coarse, dried breadcrumbs
2 tablespoons Parmesan
cheese

Melt the garlic and onion in the
olive oil in a heavy pan. Add lamb
and brown it well, turning it in
the oil. Add the aubergine, and
mix it well with the lamb and oil.
Add tomatoes, herbs, olives, seasoning. Turn all into a casserole
dish. Mix the grated cheese and
the bread crumbs together.
Sprinkle these over the top of the
mixture. Bake at 400°F. (204°C.),
gas mark 6, for 15 mins. Brown
top under grill (broiler) before
serving should this be necessary.

Serves 6.

Marinated Steak

This is delicious and, of course, the
better the steak the better the
result, but even so this is a good
way to cook a doubtful piece of
beef.

4 half-pound portions beef steak
4 small shallots
4 bay leaves
4 sprigs marjoram
For the marinade:
½ pint red wine
2 tablespoons olive oil
Lemon juice
1 garlic clove finely chopped
1 teaspoon made mustard.
I like to use French

Mix the marinade and lay the
steaks in it for at least six hours,
but overnight if possible. Really
tough steak improves if kept in the
marinade for two days.

Have ready pieces of foil for
each steak. (Incidentally, if you
use foil doubled, it is less liable to
split, can be more easily washed
and used again and again.) Take
the steaks from the marinade and
sprinkle them with lemon juice
and salt. Smear the centre of the
foil with butter and mustard.
Place a steak in the centre of each
piece. Lay a finely chopped shallot, bay leaf and marjoram on each
steak. Fold up the foil so that each
steak is firmly enveloped and no
juice can escape.

Bake at 400°F. (204°C.), gas
mark 6, for 15 mins. Unwrap each
steak on a hot plate. You will find
that there is plenty of gravy with
it but if you want more, strain the
marinade, bring to the boil, season
and thicken with a little cornflour.

Serves 4.

As you will appreciate, this is a
good recipe to use if you are
expecting guests, because so much
of it can be prepared beforehand.
You will find this way of cooking
less demanding than standing by a
grill (broiler). Just set the timer
and get on with the first course!
There is also a sense of occasion
when each steak is unwrapped
before each diner.

Chervil and Nasturtium Salad

1 cup of young nasturtium
flowers, washed, drained and
dried on paper towel. Take care
not to bruise them
1 crisp lettuce heart
1 tablespoon chopped chervil
French dressing

Line the salad bowl with the
lettuce leaves. Heap the flowers
in the centre. Sprinkle the herb on
them. Place the bowl on the table
to be admired! Mix the dressing in
well just before serving the salad.

Chives with Cooked Radishes

2 pints topped and tailed
radishes
1 oz butter
1 heaped tablespoon chopped
chives
salt and pepper

Use a heavy saucepan. Just
cover its base with water. Add the
butter and the radishes. Cover and
cook them over a low heat for 5 to
10 mins. During this time stir the
radishes occasionally with a wood-
en spoon so that all are well coated

with the liquid. Do not cook them too long; they should still be crisp when served, although they will lose their colour. Sprinkle them with the chives and seasoning and serve.

I like sometimes to stir in a little cream or cream cheese just before serving them, in which case I add the chives at the last moment so as not to drain the colour from them. If you serve these vegetables with beef, add also a little mustard to the cream.

Serves 4.

Dill Paté

This is very simply made with any canned fish, and the interesting thing is that no matter how ordinary this fish might be, guests have difficulty in identifying the taste – though appreciating the pâté none the less. For instance, a

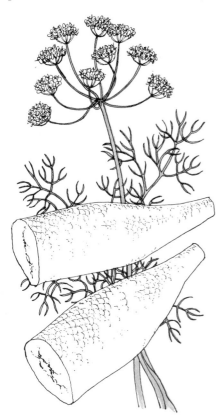

can of herrings in tomato sauce can be emptied into the mixer and made into a purée. Don't waste a scrap, empty in the entire contents. Then add lemon juice to taste – and it is wise always to keep tasting when you make dishes of this kind in which there is a product already seasoned.

Finally stir in just a sprinkling of chopped dill leaves, or should these be out of season, some of the seed. Begin with a very little, for it is easier to add more than to eliminate an over-dominant flavour. To accentuate the lemon flavour add also a little lemon thyme and/or lemon balm. Serve with crisp brown toast.

You can vary this recipe by using fennel in the same way as dill.

Serves 4.

Dill can be used with fresh or pickled seafood of any kind.

If you think of dill pickles you will realise that this herb is associated with cucumbers, but it need not be reserved for the pickled kind. It is delicious sprinkled generously over fresh-chilled cucumber in salads. Exploit this association and serve it occasionally with other members of the cucumber family, chilled cooked courgettes (or zucchini) baked squash and marrow for example.

Since I mention them, here is the recipe for

Dill Pickles

This makes just one two-pound jar of pickles.

Small, 3 inch outdoor cucumbers
1 clove garlic
6 peppercorns
1 clove
1 dill flower head
1 pint vinegar
½ pint water
1 tablespoon salt

Make sure that the jar is clean. Place the spices, dill and garlic in the jar. Wash and dry the cucumbers. Pack them well into the jar. Bring the vinegar, water and salt to the boil.

Stand the jar on a wooden board, pour in the mixture. Cover immediately.

These pickles are ready to eat after a week.

Peas, French Style

1 quart shelled peas
1 good, hearty lettuce without outside leaves, shredded
12 small onions
1 small bunch parsley and chervil
¼ lb butter
2 level teaspoons salt
4 teaspoons sugar
4 tablespoons water

Put all of these in a pan and mix well. Cover. Bring to the boil, turn down the heat and simmer them gently. When the peas are tender, take out the herbs and serve. This dish usually takes 15 to 20 mins.

Vary this by adding fennel instead of the parsley and chervil.

Mint julep (page 120): Some cool desserts for hot summer days. The herbs are mint and parsley. The desserts are two elegant mint juleps behind *two refreshing mint sorbets. On the right is a minted melon cocktail and a special preparation of candied mint. Parsley can be added as decoration.*

Stuffed Mortadella

6 thin whole slices mortadella
(salami)
3 ozs cream cheese
2 tablespoons cream
1 tablespoon freshly grated
horse-radish
1 teaspoon chervil

Mix the cream, cheese, horse-radish and chervil. Make a 'layer cake' of the mortadella, spreading the cream mixture equally between the slices. Wrap the cake in greaseproof (or waxed) paper and chill for at least an hour before serving. Cut the cake into six sections. Serve these on lettuce leaves with crusty bread.

Serves 6.

Minted Melon Cocktails

½ cup white sugar
½ cup water
3 tablespoons chopped mint
1 lemon
1 orange, both squeezed
1 good melon scooped into balls
or diced (quantities are a little
difficult here, because melons
vary so. Supply enough for six
people.)

Keep the melon in a very cool place or in the refrigerator.

Boil the sugar and water together for five minutes to make a good syrup. Pour this over the mint. Let this steep in the syrup until it cools. Strain and add to it the orange and lemon juice. Chill. Meanwhile, divide the melon into balls or dice it and share it among six tall glasses. Pour the chilled syrup over the melon. Garnish with sprigs of mint or borage.

Serves 6.

This is a refreshing first course in summer, but make sure that all is well chilled or it will seem to be too sweet.

You may not need all the syrup, but it will keep.

Those who enjoy melon at the end of a meal should consider serving this dish as a tailpiece rather than a starter.

Candied Mint Leaves

Wash the sprigs of mint carefully and shake them to remove all surplus water. Carefully pick the leaves from the stems.

Beat an egg white and coat both sides of each leaf with it, using a pastry brush. As each side is painted dip it in castor (or super-fine) sugar. Lay the leaves, well apart, on greaseproof (waxed) paper. Dry them in a slow oven, turning them from time to time.

Mint julep

Ways of preparing this famous American drink seem as personal as ways people have of making coffee. Here is a recipe passed on by a drinking friend which he swears is *the* only worthwhile recipe.

Take tall glasses. Chill them before beginning to make the drink (one way to do this is to put ice in each). Place 4 or 5 mint leaves in each glass. These must be freshly gathered. Add a teaspoon of sugar and a teaspoon of water to each glass and bruise all together using a long spoon. Have ready some crushed ice, enough

for all glasses and fill each. Pour a measure of Bourbon whisky into each glass. Stir the contents rapidly. When the level has dropped considerably, say two inches, by which time the glass should have become frosted, add more ice, refilling the glasses, and pour another measure of Bourbon into each.

Decorate the glasses with sprigs of frosted mint. (Frost these in the same way as given in the previous recipe but leave the sprigs intact. It is easiest to paint from the base of the stem to the tip.)

Stand the glasses in the refrigerator for half an hour or so before serving the drinks.

Mint Sorbet (Sherbet)

2 teaspoons powdered gelatine
2 cups of water
¾ cup sugar
2 egg whites
salt
mint

Dissolve the gelatine in four tablespoons of the water in a large basin. Boil the remaining water with the sugar. Let it boil fairly fast for ten minutes to make a good syrup. Meanwhile, chop the leaves of a good handful of mint – say about a dozen sprigs. Place these in the basin with the melted gelatine and when the syrup is ready, pour it on them. Stir the contents well and let them steep for about an hour.

Strain the syrup into a container in which it can be frozen. (I put mine straight into the freezer, using a cylindrical, lidded plastic food container). If all the sorbet (sherbet) is not used on one occasion it keeps in this container quite well. If the freezing compartment of a refrigerator is to be used, pour the syrup into trays and turn these from time to time.

Add a little green colouring if you wish, but usually enough tiny fragments of the mint are retained in the syrup to colour it well. Place the syrup in the freezer and let it partly set.

Bring it out and whisk it until it is opaque and increased in bulk. If you are freezing the sorbet in trays, make sure that the bowl is well chilled when you turn it out. The electric mixer can be used for this, but I find it is best first to beat it by hand for a while to make sure that no gelatine sticks to the bottom of the bowl.

Whisk the egg whites with a pinch of salt and fold them into the beaten syrup. All should be well blended. Return to the freezer.

To serve, shave off the sorbet by using a large metal spoon and heap it in cooled dishes. Decorate each portion with sugar-frosted, candied mint leaves and candied borage flowers. These can be coated in the same way as the mint leaves.

Fried Parsley

This makes an attractive garnish which is also good to eat. It is important that the parsley is quite dry otherwise it will splutter violently when put into the fat. It is best to wash and dry it some hours before you cook it. Pat it dry on a kitchen tissue and then let it finish in the air.

Use a frying basket and get the fat really hot with a blue haze rising above it. Lower the parsley in the basket. But be careful! The fat will hiss alarmingly. When the noise stops, lift out the basket. Drain the parsley on a paper towel. The bright green sprigs will remain crisp for some minutes.

Savory Beans with Ham

This dish can be served hot or cold.

1 quart of any freshly shelled beans
¼ pint of cream
8 slices cooked ham or thin gammon rashers
Savory, about a tablespoon

Boil the beans in salted boiling water until tender, which will be about 10 to 15 mins. Drain and dry slightly by putting the pan back over the heat. Slowly pour in the cream. Let all simmer until the cream is hot. Sprinkle in the herb finely chopped, taste, and adjust if necessary by adding more herb.

Have the meat ready on a hot dish. Divide the creamed beans so that equal portions go on each slice, to one side of it. Fold the other side over to make a 'turn-over'. Arrange nicely. Sprinkle on a little more herb as a garnish. When served hot, offer plain boiled potatoes with it. When this dish is to be served cold, allow the creamed beans to cool before putting them on the meat.

Serves 4.

Plants for the Connoisseur

Although most people grow herbs for a purely utilitarian purpose there are others who grow them simply because they are fascinated by the plants. Certainly once you delve into their histories you are inclined to view them all with a more knowing eye, and you are likely to give garden room to any that can claim the historical fame of having once been useful – if only to the Borgias.

For instance, on my herb bank grows an ever – though slowly – increasing colony of evergreen alkanet. All the plants have been produced by one poor stray I found one day growing on the edge of a lane and in danger of being crushed by farm carts once it grew to any useful size. No other plants were growing near it but when I looked over the garden wall flanking the road I could see masses of them inside in a wild border.

I have a soft spot for most plants of the boraginaceae and so I brought this one home. For years it was solitary, but now there are many. To me they symbolise the passing of winter, for it is one of the earliest true blue herbaceous flowers to bloom,

Left: Flax, Linum perenne, *has a pretty blue flower and will spread well over the ground. A decorative herb worth cultivating.*

Above: Prunella vulgaris *has a pleasant common name. It is self-heal. This is a plant that deserves and will repay much greater popularity.*

larger and bluer than forget-me-nots and smaller than anchusa.

Alkanet was once used as a dye plant, but the one I grow seems to have been a substitute. Geoffrey Grigson in his fascinating *Englishman's Flora* says that the name alkanet is a diminutive of the Spanish alcanna, which in turn comes from the Arabic al-henna, the henna plant, not the alkanet in this case but a small tree, *Lawsonia inermis*. True alkanet is *Alkanna tinctoria* and it is its roots which contain the red dye for which it was – and is – valued. The flower in my garden is *Pentaglottis sempervirens*, the evergreen alkanet, which also has blue flowers and belongs to the same family as alkanna. It also yields a dye, used by cabinet makers for staining wood.

However, I grow it for its value as a pretty garden plant as well as for a little nostalgia.

There are enough herbs, pretty, grand, unusual and just plain useful, to furnish a complete garden. Should more be necessary one could add to these the pot-pourri plants and others such as violets, jonquils, lily-of-the-valley, roses, lilies, all with sweet or memorable scents. A most unusual and delightful garden would result. As we have seen, there are plants for lawns, for carpeting, for walls, hedges, for shade and sun, for ground cover and for containers. There are also those for water.

Here are some I would choose.

Aconite, *Aconitum napellus*. Not the little yellow first-flower-of-the-year, but the tall, stately, slightly sinister and virulently poisonous (should you eat it) monkshood. Its name came from the shape of the hooded flowers. Mine grow in the shade of trees.

Agrimony, *Agrimonia eupatoria*. A British wild plant once to be found all along the waysides and now becoming rarer. Tea made from its flowering tips makes an effective gargle. The stems are slender and studded with tiny yellow blooms.

Alexanders, *Smyrnium olusatrum*. Once used widely both as a salad and as a pot herb, but superseded by celery whose taste it much resembles. In Britain it is found growing on sea cliffs. It is raised in gardens from seed.

Allspice, *Calycanthus floridus*, also called Carolina allspice. This is not the allspice of commerce which is a pepper, but a dainty shrub with fragrant wood, even more fragrant when dried and worth using for pot-pourri. It is quite hardy and easy to grow although it does best with some protection, from a south facing wall for instance.

American liverwort, *Hepatica triloba*. Many varieties with pretty anemone-like flowers in white, pink and blue which appear early in the spring.

Artemisia

Artemisia, Artemisia. This is a fairly large genus composed mainly of annuals, herbaceous perennials and shrubs, aromatic

or bitter. Some have already been mentioned and some are small enough to be grown in a rock garden. *A. abrotanum*, southern-wood, can be used to make a low, clipped hedge. The sub-shrub *A. arborescens* grows to nearly four feet. *A. camphorata* has a camphor-like pungency. *A. lanata* is beautifully downy. There are many others; enough in fact to form a collection of artemisias alone.

Autumn crocus, *Colchicum autumnale*. Not really a crocus but meadow saffron, not the saffron used in the kitchen, which comes from the saffron crocus, *Crocus sativus*. However, colchicum corms were once used in medicine. By including it in the garden one ensures a crop of beautiful chalice-like blooms in autumn, rising from the ground naked of any leaves, hence called naked ladies. The foliage follows in spring. The plant is very variable and there are some fine varieties in commerce. This is a good plant to grow under trees in partial shade or in grass.

Bistort

Bistort, *Polygonum bistorta*, snake weed. A delightful plant and one which can be left to get along on its own very well. The leaves are used for Cumberland

Easter puddings along with nettle and black currant leaves, parsley, chives, barley, oatmeal, eggs and butter.

Black Cohosh, *Cimicifuga racemosa.* The name comes from cimex, a bug, and fugo, to drive away! Good shade plant. The leafy stem grows four to eight feet tall and bears long, branched racemes of scented, creamy-white flowers. It is said to be an antidote against rattlesnake bites.

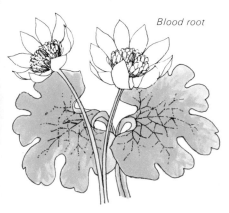
Blood root

Blood root, *Sanguinaria canadensis.* Called Indian paint because of Amer-Indians using the plant as a dye. All parts have a freely flowing orange sap. A good plant for siting under deciduous trees and in grass. It is low growing with beautiful white flowers.

Bog myrtle, *Myrica gale.* This plant has many common names, including candle berries, flea wood and sweet willow. It was once extremely common in days of early agriculture and undrained land and seems even to have been indispensable in some areas. It was used before hops were introduced for the purpose of flavouring beer. It was a dye plant, and was also used for kindling, bedding and as an insect repellant. It is a pretty, fragrant plant reminiscent of a tiny willow, with grey-green leaves and fragrant catkins in spring. It needs acid, fairly moist soil. There are other myricas including bayberry, *M. californica* and wax myrtle, *M. cerifera,* producing wax from which candles are made which burn with a sweet fragrance.

Californian sassafras, *Umbellularia californica.* An aromatic tree somewhat similar to the bay in appearance, with clusters of yellowish flowers in spring. Slightly tender, so needs protection in severe winters. The foliage is an irritant to some people.

Greater Celandine, *Chelidonium majus.* A member of the poppy family, surprisingly perhaps. Called also devil's milk and wart plant among many other folk names. The acrid, orange latex which oozes from the cut stem is applied to warts. It was once used to take the mistiness away from the eye, but mixed with other ingredients for it is very sharp. A pretty plant for the wild or woodland garden where it will soon naturalise itself.

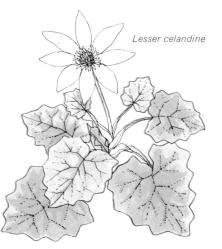
Lesser celandine

Lesser celandine, *Ranunculus ficaria,* also known as pilewort. Probably more of this plant grows in my garden than any other. It is indigenous to the locality and I have allowed it to carpet great areas which in the spring are golden with the starry flowers. They look as though each petal had been painted inside with nail varnish. By May there is no trace of the plants except for tiny tubers in the soil. These are the 'piles' or figs which because of their resemblance to that particular disorder were used in medicine and potions for its cure, whether effectively or not I cannot say.

Comfrey, *Symphytum officinale.* A handsome plant well worthy of a place in gardens. There are both white and purple forms and varieties. The plant has also crossed with imported Caucasian species, resulting in some attractive hybrids. The plant was once used as a 'knit-bone'.

Cowslip, *Primula veris.* Once a very common wild flower, but tending to disappear as methods of agriculture improve. Makes fine country wine. A syrup made of its flowers was taken to soothe the nerves. Boiled together with lavender in ale it was recommended as a cure for 'the trembelynge hand'. Seed takes a long time to germinate.

Dittany of Crete, *Origanum dictamnus.* A rather tender subshrub, suitable for the rock garden. It needs protection from the winter damp as much as from the cold.

False dittany, *Dictamnus albus,* burning bush. A scented plant with peculiar properties. Gently rub a leaf and it will impart a scent of lemon, bruise it less tenderly and it will smell of balsam. Wait until a warm, still, summer evening and hold a match over a plant and with luck the vapour from the essential oil will ignite, hence the name burning bush.

This page — Above: Dittany of Crete, Origanum dictamnus. *Right top: Alexanders,* Smyrnium olustratrum; *centre: Comfrey,* Symphytum officinale; *bottom: Cowslip,* Primula veris.

Right page — Top: Two varieties of artemisia. On the left, Artemisia schmidtii nana *and right,* Artemisia abrotanum. *Below: Autumn flowering* Colchicum maximum, *in full bloom.*

Elder, *Sambucus nigra.* Once said to have the power to ward off witches. The flowers can be used to make tea, to flavour jellies with a muscat-grape flavour, to make 'champagne', ointment for burns and cream for skin, which it makes soft and silky. Berries are used for wine and they can be used with other fruits such as blackberries and sloes in jams, jellies and pies. If you want birds to visit your garden grow an elder or two.

Elecampane, *Inula helenium.* A tall, rather coarse plant best left to the wild garden where it will look quite striking with its great 'sunflowers'. Was grown for its roots, which were candied and eaten to ease coughing and asthma. 'Wine that is every where prepar'd with this root in Germany, and often drunk, wonderfully quickens the sight.' (*The Compleat Herbal*, 1694)

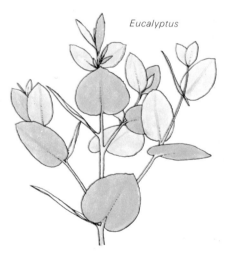
Eucalyptus

Eucalyptus species. Bruise the leaves occasionally for that evocative smell of childhood and cut and use the branches for long-lasting flower arrangements. Protect newly planted young trees with wire netting if there are rabbits in the district.

Foxglove

Foxglove, *Digitalis purpurea.* A wonderful plant for early summer. It likes acid soil so grow it with rhododendrons or in association with heathers, but do not let the seedlings smother them. It has hundreds of folk names and is associated with fairies and magic. After centuries of superstition it was found to be of great benefit to medicine, especially in the treatment of heart disease.

Heartsease, *Viola tricolor.* Once found in all old gardens. It was used in pharmacy. It is a charming little flower and once it thrives it will seed itself vigorously.

Hellebores, in variety. The roots have been used in medicine. They contain helleborin, a powerful poison. The flowers are beautiful and long lasting, blooming at a time when there are few others.

Hemp agrimony, *Eupatorium cannabinum.* A tall herbaceous plant with crushed raspberries in cream-coloured heads of flowers. Good for damp places or to grow near a stream. From it is made a tea to allay influenza.

Horehound, *Marrubium vulgare.* A good bee plant. Fresh horehound can be candied and it is also used in making ale. Was once used as a culinary herb but modern palates find its taste too strong.

Hound's tongue, *Cynoglossom officinale.* A biennial, a pretty member of the borage family, but with a strange odour. Once used for many purposes, for burns, sores, and even, if worn in the shoes, to prevent dogs barking at you!

Houseleek, *Sempervivum tectorum.* Known also as St. Patrick's cabbage and Welcome-home-husband - however - drunk - and - late - you - may - be; this plant has received more common names than all the other sempervivums put together. It was said to be a magical plant which would protect a house against lightning. Consequently it was also used for cooling burns, soothing ulcers and the like. In the garden it can be very variable. An attractive plant for the rock garden, for paving and for containers.

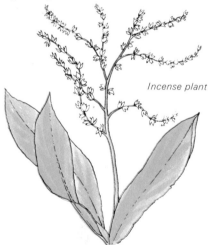
Incense plant

Incense plant, *Humea elegans.* A biennial usually grown as a greenhouse plant for its aromatic foliage, but it can be planted outdoors in summer where it must be strongly staked against winds because it is feathery and frail in spite of its height.

Indian ginger, *Asarum canadense*, also Canadian snake root. An unusual and hardy plant for the woodland garden, although it can be grown on some rock gardens. It has large leaves and solitary flowers. The root is aromatic, spicy and ginger-like to taste. Dried it has stimulative and carminative properties.

Insect powder plants

Insect powder plants, *Chrysanthemum cinerariifolium* and *C. roseum.* The first is a little yellow-eyed daisy and the other rose-red or flesh-coloured. The flower heads should be picked as they are ready to open and dried. They may then be ground to a powder and used as a safe insecticide, even on plants to be eaten such as lettuce. The powder can also be put into sachets and used to repel clothes moths.

Jacob's ladder, *Polemonium caeruleum.* Once used to heal cuts, it is worth growing in a garden simply because it is so pretty. The stem is erect and grows as much as two and a half feet, with leaves so placed that they give the name 'ladder' to the plant. Flowers are blue, rarely white.

Jerusalem sage

Jerusalem sage, *Phlomis fruticosa.* A handsome plant and one which figures importantly in my main silver border. The leaves are aromatic and can be used in pot-pourris. The seed heads are attractive and useful in flower arrangements.

Labrador tea, *Ledum groenlandicum.* A small, evergreen, upright shrub whose leaves are fragrant when bruised. Tea made from the leaves which have a spicy taste is recommended for easing coughs and dyspepsia.

Lady's mantle, *Alchemilla mollis.* This is a must in any garden, herbal or general. The name comes from alkemelych, the Arabic name for the plant, and derived from the same root as alchemy, the little magical one. Obviously it was once of great importance, and today it is beloved especially by gardeners and flower arrangers. There are other species, all worth growing. I grow *A. alpina* in the foreground of my silver border. It is also a good and effective rock garden plant.

Lavender, lavendula species There are many lavenders. Varieties that come to mind quickly include the pretty little dwarf Twickle Purple, which I grow. It has the best scent of all the dwarf kinds and it is a good strong colour. Over the years it has made a thick little bush of some two feet in height. It makes a good dwarf hedge.

There are others even dwarfer, including the pretty little pink lavender, *L. spica nana rosea. L. spica* has produced many varieties including *alba*, white, *gigantea*, usually sold as Grappenhall variety, the strongest growing variety, and Munstead Dwarf. *L. lanata* is woolly with very fragrant flowers.

Lavender stoechas

L. stoechas is a little oddity, a shrub up to three feet tall with a peculiar inflorescence crowned with a cluster of bracts.

If a collection of lavenders appeals to you it is well worth searching nurseries, garden centres and gardens for unusual types even if these vary only a little from the species. There are also other species, not all of them sweetly fragrant.

Some of the less common herbs make colourful, and useful, additions to any garden. Top left: Lady's mantle, Alchemilla mollis. Top right: Elecampane, Inula helenium. *Bottom left: Pansy or Heartsease, Viola tricolor. Bottom right: Elder, Sambucus nigra. Far right: The beautiful flower of houseleek, Sempervivum.*

Linseed, *Linum usitatissimum,* common flax. Having once seen fields of flax in bloom, matching the summer skies above them, I am never likely to forget that this is one of the real blue flowers; pale, unlike the bolder blue of cornflowers, but well worth growing. It is annual, and is easily raised from seed. It was once grown for its fibres from which linen was made, and for its oils and seeds, which were made into poultices and teas taken for coughs.

Lion's tail, *Agastache mexicana.* A perennial with pleasantly aromatic, soft grey-green leaves. The flowers, rose to crimson, grow in whorls. Another from the same family, *A. anisata,* is known also as the anise hyssop. This grows to three feet, a few inches taller than lion's tail. Its leaves are downy on the underside and scented of anise. The flowers are blue.

Liquorice

Liquorice, *Glycyrrhiza glabra.* The sweet roots are the source of liquorice. The plant grows from about three to four feet tall, is a perennial and a member of the pea family with pinnate leaves. Flowers are pale blue.

Lungwort

Lungwort, *Pulmonaria officinalis.* Also called, among other names, soldiers and sailors, because the flowers are 'redcoats' and 'bluecoats' together on the same plant. As its name indicates the plant was once used to aid pulmonary troubles. With its prettily spotted, hairy leaves, the plant needs a soil which remains fairly moist at all times.

Mace, *Achillea decolorans.* This is not the mace of commerce. The scent of its leaves is said to resemble this spice and they are sometimes used to flavour certain soups and stews. The flower heads are in corymbs, yellowish-white on stems about a foot tall. The leaves are both glabrous and toothed. There is a double variety. See also Yarrow.

Mallows, *Malva.* Members of the hollyhock family once used for poultices, ointments and soothing syrups for coughs, among other things. The common mallow, *Malva sylvestris,* produces round, flat discs of seeds which some country children call 'cheeses.' They taste rather like peanuts.

The plants are somewhat coarse and need plenty of room.

M. moschata is the musk mallow.

Marjoram species. Although this plant has already been described, I cannot forbear to give a reminder that the golden form is really very beautiful. Planted at the edge of a sunny border and near a path it will spill over very prettily.

Mints

Mints. The collector can really go to town on mints. There are, for instance, many forms of hybrids between *M. longifolia* and *M. rotundifolia,* known as *M. x alopecuroides,* resembling a fox's brush, a description which refers to the young flower stems, stout hairy spikes one and a half to two inches long and lengthening as they age.

There are also Japanese mint, *M. arvensis piperascens,* tall and downy and a source of menthol; *M. citrata,* with synonyms *M. odorata* and *M. aquatica citrata,* fragrantly lemon-scented; *M. piperata,* peppermint, with its varieties; *M. pulegium,* pennyroyal, a prostrate creeping variety with use as a carpeting plant which also has a variegated form known as Gibraltar mint; and yet others.

Motherwort, *Leonurus cardiaca.* Extremely rare in the wild, so search for a plant among gardening friends or from a specialist herb nursery. It was respected during the Middle Ages as a plant to be used for women in difficult labour and for heart troubles. It is decorative, a labiate, but with uncharacteristic maple-like leaves. It produces spires of tall, mauve-pink flowers.

Mountain tobacco, *Arnica montana.* Prettiest when growing in the mountains, but sometimes quite delightful on a rock garden.

Mullein, *Verbascum thapsus.* In addition to the further names of Aaron's rod and Adam's flannel there are plenty more so you can take your pick. A handsome, woolly plant, so woolly in fact that the down was once collected and used for lamp wicks. The yellow flowers stud the downy stem which grows about three feet tall. A delightful plant anywhere, but especially good for a silver border.

Myrtle

Myrtle, *Myrtus communis.* A pretty evergreen shrub with tiny leaves, but not quite hardy. It needs the shelter of a south wall and it will not thrive outdoors in cold areas. I have found it easy to raise from seed. There are varieties, including a variegated form.

Our lady's milk thistle, *Silybum marianum.* The white splotches on the large prickly leaves are Mary's milk according to an ancient belief. The plant was formerly grown for food, its roots boiled and used in soups and stews, the heads eaten like artichokes and the young leaves as salad. It was also considered a balm against melancholy.

Periwinkle

Periwinkle, *Vinca minor* and *V. major.* Other names include sorcerer's violet and all-heal, names that hint at the plant's history. These are excellent plants for covering large areas of soil, but invasive if planted in borders. They are good also for binding the soil on a bank. There are many varieties of *V. minor,* with flowers that differ in colour from the species. Some are double. There are also variegated forms of both plants. Varieties are interesting enough to make a collection.

Poke weed, *Phytolacca americana.* Also pigeon berry and red ink plant. Handsome, but to me at least, sinister as poisonous plants so frequently are, although the young shoots have been used as pot herbs. It is the dark berries forming the long 'pokes' which are poisonous.

Red-root, *Ceanothus americanus.* Also known as New Jersey tea because the leaves were used as a substitute during the American war of independence. It appears to have been a useful plant, providing dyes, gargles and cures for bronchitis and asthma. The new shoots are downy and the leaves have downy undersides. Flowers are generously produced in panicles of grey-white, which with the leaves gives the plant an overall silvery appearance.

Rosemary

Rosemary, Rosemarinus. As I mentioned in an earlier chapter, the *R. officinalis* has many varieties, including one with white flowers, *albiflorus* or *albus. R. erectus* also known as *fastigiatus* or *pyramidalis,* grows tall and erect, while *humilis* lives up to its name by spreading its branches in a low curtsey. There is also a *prostratus,* which is known more correctly botanically as *R. lavandulaceus,* and is not quite hardy.

*Above top: Our Lady's milk
thistle*, Silybum marianum. *Above:
Mullein,* Verbascum bombyciferum.
Left: Poke weed, Phytolacca
clavigera. *Right: Common mallow,*
Malva sylvestris.

Roses. Of these I wish just to say that any spaces in your all-herb garden can be filled with any of the scented roses, either 'wild' by which I mean the species, or the old-fashioned cultivars. They also can be made to cover walls, paths and arbours.

Rue

Rue, *Ruta graveolens.* Herb of grace, including a lovely variegated form. This is one of my favourite scented plants, for not only does it furnish the garden so handsomely but it is also fine for flower arrangements.

Although it was once used as a tonic in the form of rue tea, as a stimulant and to dispel headaches in man and croup in poultry, there are some people who are fiercely allergic to the plant.

Sages, salvia species. I have already sung many praises to these plants. The common sage, *S. officinalis*, has many varieties, the most vividly coloured of which is *tricolor*, in which plant you are actually likely to find more than three hues. It seems to me that each time I wander around a garden centre I find yet another form of decorative sage.

S. rutilans, half-hardy, is the pineapple scented sage.

Samphire, *Crithmum martimum.* The generic name comes from krithe, barley, an allusion to the shape of its seed, while the common name originated from *herbe de St. Pierre*, the fisherman saint. This is a sea cliff plant and not always easy to grow inland, although it has been done and in fact it was once a common kitchen garden plant. It is best to collect seed and sow it as soon as it is ripe. Give the plant sun, warmth, a dry position, a well drained soil and some protection in winter. Because the plant grew from rock it was once also used against kidney stones and other bladder complaints. Samphire can be pickled, made into sauces with butter and cooked and eaten cold as a salad.

Self heal, *Prunella vulgaris.* The name gives a clue to its use, for it comes from *brunella* from the German term for quinsy, *die Braiine*. I found some growing in the grass in my own garden, so uprooted it and put it on the herb bank in a moist and shady spot, where it flourishes. It can be a troublesome weed in a good lawn, but if you are searching for creeping plants that will make a non-grass lawn, this is one of them. The flowers are short-stemmed, whorled in spikes, usually purple but sometimes pink or white.

Soapwort

Soapwort, *Saponaria officinalis*, or bouncing Bet. A laundry plant, from sapo, soap, once used to make a lather, now an ingredient in a solution in which old tapestries and fabrics can be cleaned and sometimes their colours restored. A pretty plant, but I have found it very invasive. It needs a space to itself.

Sweet flag, *Acorus calamus.* A plant which is fragrant in all its parts. Oelum calami is an oil extracted from its roots and used in perfumery. Best grown as a bog plant or in moist, loamy soil. There is a pleasant variegated form, *variegatus*, with cream and gold stripes.

Thorn apple

Thorn apple, *Datura stramonium.* An annual often found naturalised. Its specific name proves its worth, for this plant renders stramonium, used in pharmacy. It is a strange, almost macabre plant to study and has given rise to many myths, notably that to fall asleep in its shade was to invite death because you would be breathing in the poisons exhaled by the plant. It has narcotic properties. The leaves are blended into a suitable mixture for igniting to make a vapour to relieve asthma.

Thymes, thymus species. There are so many of these that you

Thymes

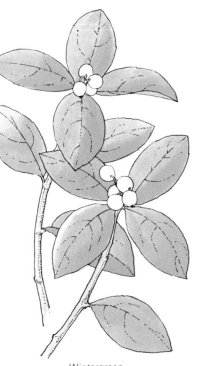

Wintergreen

Yarrow

Woad, *Isatis tinctoria.* Common dyer's weed, a biennial which grows two to four feet tall. Worth growing simply because it is a relic of older days. Grow it in a mass to get clouds of yellow, honey-scented flowers with glaucous leaves. It will grow in any ordinary but good garden soil.

could fill a garden with them. The plants are sometimes difficult to classify, a fact recognised and deplored by many botanists. There are many hybrids, not all of them recognised as such. When bruised the various plants produce aromas which can be compared to those of lemon, camphor, turpentine, caraway and others.

Tree germander, *Teucrium fruticans.* A half-hardy shrub with silver-grey foliage, not unlike rosemary at first glance, particularly when it is in flower. Pleasantly scented. Other teucriums are wall germander, *T. chamaedrys* and wood sage or sage-leaved germander, *T. scorodonia.* Cat thyme is *T. marum.*

Valerian, *Valeriana officinalis.* From valere, to be healthy. Also called all-heal. A common plant in the wild in Europe. The roots are edible, and dried they will attract a cat. Once these roots were used as a linen herb (their smell is like new leather and is called phu) no doubt because a nervine can be produced from them which is said to induce sleep.

Wintergreen, *Gaultheria procumbens.* Wintergreen or checkerberry, a pretty creeping or spicy decorative low-growing shrub not unlike the pernettya and needing the same lime-free soil. The white flowers are followed by red fruits. Young leaves are nicely bronzed as well as fragrant. The fragrance may seem familiar to some, for oil of wintergreen is used to flavour some toothpastes as well as an ingredient in liniments.

Witch hazel, *Hamamelis virginiana.* The source of bay rum. From this plant also is made a lotion used for soothing the skin. The shrubs are fun in a garden because they bloom so early, the odd little yellow bloom tassels decorating the branches long before the leaves appear. There are other species including the very fragrant *H. japonica,* which has given rise to many varieties.

Yarrow, *Achillea millefolium.* A mat-forming plant with pretty feathery leaves. It can be the despair of those who are proud of their lawns, but worth growing if you want a carpeting plant, and a good plant for borders if kept under strict control. The wild species has white flowers, sometimes rose. The rosea varieties vary and have given rise to a good garden form, Cerise Queen. It was once principally a wound healer and considered powerful against evil.

Yerba buena, *Micromeria chamissonia.* Also called *M. douglassi* and *Thymus chamissonis,* one of the fragrant members of this genus. Among others are *M. corsica,* with thyme-like flowers and oddly scented, with a fragrance hard to define or to describe, and *M. piperella,* sometimes called *T. piperella,* with a peppery scent attractive to cats. Not really wholly hardy.

Top left: A garden variety of Achillea millefolium. *Top right: Once used as a body-stain, Woad, or* Isatiş tinctoria *is still worth growing.*

Above: The well-named 'Ruby Glow', Hamamelis mollis x intermedia. *Right: The subtle shade of colour in the flower of* Saponaria officinalis.

The Names of the Herbs

The common names for the Latin terms.

Look on this page if you know only the Latin name of a herb and want to know the common name. Look in the Index if you know the common name and want to know the Latin name.

A

Achillea millefolium	Yarrow
Agrimonia eupatoria	Agrimony
Alchemilla mollis	Lady's Mantle
Alkanna tinctoria	Alkanet
Allium ascalonicum	Shallots
Allium sativum	Garlic
Allium schoenoprasum	Chives
Althea officinalis	Marsh Mallow
Andropogon squarrosus	Khus-Khus, also called Cus-Cus, Vetiver and Vetivert
Angelica archangelica	Angelica
Anthemis nobilis	Camomile
Anthriscus cerefolium	Chervil
Artemisia abrotanum	Southernwood, also called Lad's Love
Artemisia absinthium	Wormwood
Artemisia dracunculus	Tarragon
Artemisia vulgaris	Mugwort
Asperula odorata	Woodruff

B

Betonica officinalis	Betony
Borago officinalis	Borage

C

Calendula officinalis	Pot Marigold
Carum carvi	Caraway
Chrysanthemum balsamita	Alecost, also called Costmary
Chrysanthemum cinerariifolium	Insect Powder Plant
Chrysanthemum roseum	Insect Powder Plant
Chelidonium majus	Greater Celandine
Colchicum autumnale	Autumn Crocus
Coriandrum sativum	Coriander
Cuminum cyminum	Cumin

E

Eupatorium cannabinum	Hemp Agrimony

F

Filipendula ulmaria	Meadowsweet
Foeniculum vulgare	Fennel

G

Gaultheria procumbens	Wintergreen
Geranium pratense	Meadow Crane's Bill

H

Humea elegans	Incense Plant
Hyoscyamus niger	Henbane
Hyssopus officinalis	Hyssop

I

Inula helenium	Elecampane
Iris florentina	Orris
Isatis tinctoria	Woad

L

Laurus nobilis	Bay
Lavendula officinalis	Lavender
Leonurus cardiaca	Motherwort
Ligusticum scoticum	Lovage
Linum usitatissimum	Linseed, also called Common Flax
Lippia citriodora	Lemon Verbena

M

Malva sylvestris	Common Mallow
Marubium vulgare	Horehound
Melilotus officinalis	Melilot
Melissa officinalis	Balm, also called Melissa, Lemon Balm

Mentha sp.	*Mints*
Mentha piperata	*Peppermint*
Mentha pulegium	*Pennyroyal*
Mentha rotundifolia	*Applemint*
Mentha spicata	*Spearmint*
Monarda didyma	*Bergamot*
Myrrhis odorata	*Sweet Cicely, also called Spanish Chervil, Giant Sweet Chervil, Myrrh*
Myrtus communis	*Myrtle*

N

Nepeta cataria	*Catmint, also called Catnip*

O

Ocimum basilicum	*Sweet Basil*
Ocimum minimum	*Bush Basil*
Origanum sp.	*Marjorams*
Origanum dictamnus	*Dittany of Crete*
Origanum marjorana	*Sweet Marjoram, also called Knotted Marjoram*
Origanum onites	*Pot Marjoram*

P

Pelargonium graveolens	*Rose Geranium*
Petroselinum crispum	*Parsley*
Peucedanum graveolens	*Dill*
Philadelphus coronarius	*Mock Orange*
Phlomis fruticosa	*Jerusalem Sage*
Phytolacca clavigera	*Poke Weed*
Pimpinella anisum	*Anise*
Polygonum bistorta	*Bistort*
Prunella vulgaris	*Self-Heal*
Pulmonaria officinalis	*Lungwort*

R

Ranunculus ficaria	*Lesser Celandine*
Reseda odorata	*Mignonette*
Rosmarinus officinalis	*Rosemary*
Rosmarinus pyramidalis	*Rosemary*
Rumex acetosa	*Sorrel*
Ruta graveolens	*Rue*

S

Salvia officinalis	*Sage*
Sambucus nigra	*Elder*
Sanguinaria canadensis	*Blood Root*
Sanguisorba minor	*Salad Burnet*
Santolina chamaecyparissus	*Cotton Lavender, also called Santolina*
Saponaria officinalis	*Soapwort*
Satureia hortensis	*Summer Savory*
Satureia montana	*Winter Savory*
Sempervivum tectorum	*Houseleek*
Silybum marianum	*Our Lady's Milk Thistle*
Smyrnium olustratrum	*Alexanders*
Symphytum officinale	*Comfrey*

T

Tanacetum vulgare	*Tansy*
Teucrium sp.	*Germander*
Thymus vulgaris	*Thyme*
Thymus x citriodorus	*Lemon Thyme*
Tilia europea	*Lime*
Tropaeolum majus	*Nasturtium*

V

Verbascum bombyciferum	*Mullein*
Vinca minor	*Periwinkle*
Vinca major	*Periwinkle*
Viola odorata	*Violet*
Viola tricolor	*Pansy, also called Heartsease*

Index

A

Aconite, also called Monkshood, *Aconitum napellus*; 124

Agrimony, *Agrimonia eupatoria*; 124

Alecost, also called Costmary, Sweet Mary, Bible Leaf, *Chrysanthemum balsamita*; cooking, 90–91; drying, 53; growing, 90–91; other uses, 45, 54, 56, 57, 90

Alexanders, *Smyrnium olustratrum*; 124, *126*

Alkanet, *Alkanna tinctoria*; 124

Alkanet, Evergreen, *Pentaglottis sempervirens*; 123–124

Allspice, *Calycanthus floridus*; 124

Ambrosia, also called Mexican Tea, *Chcnopodium ambrosioides*; 48

American Liverwort, *Hepatica triloba*; 124

Angelica, *Angelica archangelica*; 7, 75–76, *75*; cooking, 75–76; drying, 53; growing, 19, 24, 34, 76; other uses, 40, 48, 54, 56

Anise, *Pimpinella anisum*; *76*; cooking, 77; growing, 25, 77; other uses, 77

Anise Chervil. See Sweet Cicely

Applemint, (See also Mints) *Mentha rotundifolia*; cooking, 82, 83; growing, 82–84, 132; other uses, 56

Artemisia, Artemisia sp.; 49, *124*, *127*; growing, 124

Aubergine. See Egg-Plant

Autumn Crocus. See Colchicum

B

Balm, also called Melissa, Lemon Balm, *Melissa officinalis*; *87*; cooking, 86, *106–107*, 117; drying, 49; growing, 20, 29, *36*, 86–88; other uses, 48, 49, 60, 62, 86

    Golden Balm, *Melissa officinalis aurea*; 88

Balsams; 40, 62

Basil, Ocimum sp.

    Bush Basil, *Ocimum minimum*; cooking, 84; growing, 25, 29, 30, 32, 34, 84; other uses, 84

    Sweet Basil, *Ocimum basilicum*; *83*; cooking, 84, 105, 108, 113; growing, 25, 29, 30, 32, 34, *36*, 84; other uses, 49, 84

Baths; 60

Bath bag; 60

Bay, *Laurus nobilis*; 2, *95*, *99*; cooking, 67, 95–96, *102*, *106–107*, 108, 112–113, *115*, 116; drying, *99*, 100; growing, 20, *20*, 22, 24, 27, 95–96; other uses, 49, 54, 56

Bergamot (Mint), *Mentha citrata*; cooking, 88; growing, 89

Bergamot (Sweet), *Monarda didyma, 88*; cooking, 88–89; growing, *36, 46*, 89; other uses, 45, 60, 65, 88–89

Betony, *Betonica officinalis*; 15

Bible Leaf. See Alecost

Bistort, *Polygonum bistorta*; *124*, 124–125

Black Cohosh, *Cimicifuga racemosa*; 125

Blood Root, *Sanguinaria canadensis*; *125*, 125

Bog Myrtle. See Myrtle

Borage, *Borago officinalis*; cooking, 96, 105, 108, 112, 113, 120; drying, 100; growing, 20, 25, *36*, 96; other uses, 46, 96

Bouquet Garni; 108

British or European Thyme. See Thyme

Bush Basil. See Basil

Butters; 104

C

Californian Sassafras, *Umbellularia californica*; 125

Camomile, *Anthemis nobilis*; *91*, 91–92; growing, 19, 92; other uses, 12, 46, 60, 62, 65

Candied Mint Leaves; *118–119*, 120

Candied Violets; 65

Capers; 108

Caraway, *Carum carvi*; *76*; cooking, 69, 72, 112; drying, 77; growing, 25, 77; other uses, 65, 77

Carnations, Dianthus sp.; 44–45; growing, 45; other uses, 44–45, 56

Carrots; cooking, 69, 70

Catmint, also called Catnip, *Nepeta cataria*; 49, *49*, 65

Cat toys; 64–65

Celandine, Greater, *Chelidonium majus*; 125

Celandine, Lesser, *Ranunculus ficaria*; *125*, 125

Celery; cooking, 69

Cherry Pie, Heliotrope sp., *Heliotrope peruvianum*; 46 *Heliotrope corymbosum*; 46

Chervil, *Anthriscus cerefolium*; *72*; cooking, 69, 72, 89, 105, *106–107*, 108, 112, 113, *115*, 116, 117, 120; drying, 100; growing, 21, *23*, 25, 72

Chervil and Nasturtium Salad; 116

Chicory, *Cichorium intybus*; 14

Chives, *Allium schoenoprasum*; *94*, 95, *110*; cooking, 89, 92, 94–95, *102*, 105, *106–107*, 108, 109, 113, 116, 117, 125; drying, 100; growing, 20, 22, 24, 25, *27*, 27, 28, 29, 30, 32, 34, 36, 95

Chives with Cooked Radishes; 116–117

Cinnamon; 53, 54, 56, 57, 62

Citrus Peel; 40, 53, 56

Clary, *Salvia sclarea*; 46

Cloves; 62, *114–115*; cooking, 117; other uses, 53, 54, 56, 57, 62

Cocktails, Minted Melon; 120

Colchicum, also called Autumn crocus *Colchicum autumnale*; 124 *Colchicum maximum*; *127*

Comfrey, *Symphytum officinale*; *125* 126

Common Mallow. See Mallow

Compositae; 89

Compost; 32, 34

Condiments; 109

Containers, or Pots; *28, 29*, 30

Coriander, *Coriandrum sativum*; 13, 77; cooking, 77–78, 108; drying, 52, 77–78; growing, 25, 77–78; other uses, 53, 54, 56, 57, 77–78

Corsage; 64

Costmary. See Alecost

Cotton Lavender, also called Santolina, *Santolina chamaecyparissus*; *19*, *49*, 49, 61

Cowslip, *Primula veris*; 125, *126*

Cumin, *Cuminum cyminum*; *79*; cooking, 69, 78; drying, 78; growing, 25, 78, 112

Curry Plant, *Helichrysum angustifolium*; *23*, 46

Cus-Cus. See Khus-Khus

Custard, Marigold; 112

Custard, Baked Savoury; 112

D

Delphinium: 45

Dill, *Peucedanum graveolens*; *74*; cooking, 69, 74–75, *106–107*, 113, *114*, 117; growing, 25, *36*, 75; other uses, 75

Dill Paté; 117

Dill Pickles; 113, 117

Dittany of Crete. See Marjorams

Drying; 57, *99*, *100*, *101*, 99–101; flowers, 53; leaves, 53

E

Egg-Plant, also called Aubergine; cooking, 80, *114–115*, 116

Elder, *Sambucus nigra*; 128, 130

Elecampane, *Inula helenium*; 128, *130*

Escoffier Mayonnaise; 108

Eucalyptus; *128*, 128

European Marjoram. See Marjorams

European Mint. See Mints

F

False Capers. See Nasturtium

False Dittany, *Dictamnus albus*; 125

Fines Herbes; 104

Fennel, Foeniculum sp. *Foeniculum vulgare*; *73, 110*; cooking, 9, 67, 69, 72–74, 80, *102–103*, 105, 108, 109, 112, *114–115*, 117; drying, 100; growing, 21, 24, 28, 29, 30, *67*, 74; other uses, 12, 65

    Florence Fennel, also called Sweet Fennel, Finnochio, *Foeniculum vulgare* var. *dulce*; 74, 100; cooking, 11, 69, 72–74; growing, 74

    Giant Fennel, *Foeniculum officinalis*; 25, 100

    Italian Fennel, *Foeniculum vulgare* var. *piperitum*; 74, 100

    Sweet Fennel, See Florence Fennel

Finnochio. See Florence Fennel

Fixatives; 40, 62

Flax, *Linum perenne*; *122*

Flax, Common. See Linseed

Flowers; for pot-pourri, 43–48; drying, 53; in vinegars, 56

Forget-me-nots; 62

Foxglove, *Digitalis purpurea*; *9, 128*, 128

French Parsley, See Parsley

G

Garlic, *Allium sativum*; *93, 110*; cooking, 9, 70, 92, 105, 108, 109, *114–115*, 116, 117; drying, 92; growing, 25, 92

Garlic Vinegar; 109

Geranium, Geranium sp.; *49*, 49, *50–51*

Geranium, Oak-leaved, *Pelargonium quercifolium*; 52

Germander, Teucrium sp.; 137

    Tree Germander, *Teucrium fruticans*; 137

Giant Fennel. See Fennel

Giant Sweet Chervil. See Sweet Cicely

Golden Balm. See Balm

PDO 81-261